A SAMPLER OF

The Virtue of Humility
"For the most part I do what my own nature prompts me to do. It is embarrassing to earn so much respect and love for it." —Albert Einstein

The Virtue of Integrity
"What you are speaks so loudly I can't hear what you're saying."   —Ralph Waldo Emerson

The Virtue of Perseverance
"The sense of obligation to continue is present in all of us. A duty to strive is the duty of us all. I felt a call to that duty."

—Abraham Lincoln

The Virtue of Trust
"Those who wait for the Lord shall renew their strength, they shall mount up with wings like eagles, they shall run and not be weary, they shall walk and not faint."   —Isaiah Yo

LINDA KAVELIN POPOV is president of the Virtues Project, Inc. She is a psychotherapist, organizational consultant, former hospice spiritual care director, and mother. She facilitates community healing and development throughout the world and speaks internationally on the cultivation of personal and corporate virtues. She is also the co-author of *The Family Virtues Guide*, which is available in a Plume edition.

SACRED MOMENTS

*Daily Meditations
on the Virtues*

Linda Kavelin Popov

A PLUME BOOK

PLUME
Published by the Penguin Group
Penguin Putnam Inc., 375 Hudson Street,
New York, New York 10014, U.S.A.
Penguin Books Ltd, 27 Wrights Lane, London W8 5TZ, England
Penguin Books Australia Ltd, Ringwood, Victoria, Australia
Penguin Books Canada Ltd, 10 Alcorn Avenue,
Toronto, Ontario, Canada M4V 3B2
Penguin Books (N.Z.) Ltd, 182–190 Wairau Road,
Auckland 10, New Zealand

Penguin Books Ltd, Registered Offices:
Harmondsworth, Middlesex, England

Published by Plume, an imprint of Dutton Signet,
a member of Penguin Putnam Inc.
Originally published by Virtues Communications, Inc.

First Plume Printing, October, 1997
10 9 8 7 6 5 4 3 2 1

 REGISTERED TRADEMARK—MARCA REGISTRADA

LIBRARY OF CONGRESS CATALOGING-IN-PUBLICATION DATA
Popov, Linda Kavelin.
    Sacred moments : daily meditations on the virtues / Linda
Kavelin Popov.
        p.   cm.
    ISBN 0-452-27811-2
    1. Virtues.   2. Devotional calendars. I. Title.
BJ1531.P66   1997
242'.2—dc21
                                                97–17813
                                                CIP
Printed in the United States of America

DEDICATION

I dedicate *Sacred Moments* to my children,
Christopher and Craig. The purity of your true
natures has always inspired my reverence.

CONTENTS

CONTENTS

CONTENTS

ACKNOWLEDGMENTS

I want to acknowledge my heartfelt thanks to my husband, Dan, for thoughtfully and creatively setting up the writing corner where *Sacred Moments* was developed and for his steadfast research in the sacred texts of the world's religions; to my brother, John Kavelin, for his creative input to the interior design; to Patrick Falso for titling the book; to my friend, Dr. David Baker, for his instant enthusiasm in agreeing to be my research assistant and for so lovingly and reverently extracting the choicest gems from many volumes; to Janet Luhrs and Leslie Campbell for their truthful and discerning editorial comments and for taking the time to review the manuscript in the midst of all their other publishing and creative priorities; to my assistant, Karen Shergold, for her unabashed enthusiasm for all my projects and able assistance in gathering the many permissions needed for the material included in the book; and finally, to my editor at Plume, Deb Brody for her wise guidance and her grace under pressure.

INTRODUCTION

Sacred Moments is intended to help you spend a little sacred time each day reflecting on your virtues, the gifts within your soul.

Virtues are the essence of soulfulness. They are a great mystery because they are both within us and beyond us. They are described by all cultures and religions as both the qualities of the Divinity and the simple elements of the human soul, the qualities of character which reflect the "image and likeness" of God. An act of love, or justice, or creativity or any of our other virtues is essentially an expression of our spirituality.

The First Century Christian angelologist, Dionysius, Bishop of Athens, identified virtues as a very high order of angels, which are the teachers and guides for both the archangels and for the guardian angels watching over humanity. In other religious traditions, virtues are described as direct emanations of the Creator, or sub-personalities of the Holy Spirit. Virtues are the link between the human and the Divine nature. Sometimes, they are the missing link.

One of the clearest definitions of virtue I have ever heard was from a six-year-old girl who said, "Virtues are what's good about us." I think of virtues as the gems hidden in the mine of the true self. Unless we see them, name them and use them, they are lost to us, although they are always waiting, like treasures to be found. But it takes some digging.

A few days before my father died in 1988, he said to me, "Lin, be yourself. Be yourself." "What do you mean, Dad?" I asked him, a bit puzzled. "Do you think I'm not myself?" "No," he said, "but sometimes you're more than yourself." I have reflected on my father's words many times and have come to see that he was calling me to Purity, to live truly my own nature. What is "more than" is the extraneous—the fears, illusions, the drivenness, the attachments which cloud my vision or distract me from my natural Gentleness, Trust, and Peacefulness. But how does one stop being "more than" and become true to the virtues of the Self? I believe it is by cultivating the virtues. It is much easier to *do* something than to stop doing something, for example, to focus on forgiveness rather than to stop feeling resentful.

Several years ago, my husband, Dan Popov, a pediatric clinical psychologist, my brother John Kavelin, a designer with the Walt Disney Company, and I asked the question, "What can we do to make a difference?" Upon reflection, we felt called to work with virtues. I have since learned that that call was heard by others—writers, educators, healers—perhaps as a message from the spiritual realm to humanity saying "It's time to remember who you are."

My work as a founder of The Virtues Project takes me throughout the world, speaking to people of many cultures about how to cultivate the virtues which are the expression of their true selves. Whether speaking with Maori elders in New Zealand, middle-class parents in Portland or Dallas, high school students in Cyprus, or corporate executives in Vancouver, I see the same "Aha!" response. Virtues *are* what's best about us. They are a way of life, a language, a context for lived spirituality.

It is my hope that you will use *Sacred Moments* as a tool to help you create some sacred time each day in which to explore your own virtues. I suggest that you read slowly and contemplatively, spending a few unhurried moments reading one page per day and meditating on the affirmation or reflection questions of the day. A journal to record the insights which come to you would be a good companion in this process.

There are 52 virtues in this book, one for each week. People have asked me "How did you select these particular virtues and why are they in the order they are in?" The selection and order of the virtues came as a result of prayerful discernment. The first virtue, Discernment, came immediately when the idea for the book took shape. After researching and writing the chapter on that virtue, I held the question lightly in meditation, "What virtue is next?" and when it came to mind, I went on to research it. It was fascinating to me that the last virtue to be discerned was Contentment, a virtue which until now has eluded me. I can honestly say that since completing the book, my own contentment has deepened. May it be the same for you.

Seven days are devoted to each virtue in order to bring a few of its many facets to light. Day One of each virtue contains a poem, a meditation or a story, a few of which are about people you will recognize. Most come out of my own experiences: with the dying as a hospice Spiritual Care Director, with psychotherapy clients, virtues seminars, First Nations healing retreats, my family and friends. The most intimate pieces of all are about my own prayer life. I dare to disclose these personal stories only because of a deep desire to help others expand their own awareness of the possibilities which meditating on the virtues holds for them.

A word about the quotations. Many of them are from the sacred texts of the world's religions, the primary source of humanity's collective knowledge about the virtues. It is interesting to note, in light of the frequent use of male pronouns, that in many of the original languages in which these texts were written, such as Aramaic and Arabic, the referents are gender-neutral.

This book started out to be much wordier, more explanatory. I heard in meditation one day, "Simply less". My guidance was strongly affirmed later that day by a letter from my editor saying exactly the same thing. It is my sincere hope that, whatever your own beliefs or practices, this simple book will be an enjoyable addition to your spiritual tool kit.

—LINDA KAVELIN POPOV

SACRED MOMENTS

THE VIRTUE OF DISCERNMENT

January 1

Su and Dave take time each summer to sail up the coast of British Columbia. Their house is ornamented with treasures of simple beauty gleaned from the shores they have explored—a conch in shades of rose and pearl on a table beside some books; three smooth, perfect stones arranged by size on a porch step; a bowl of sand with circles raked around a single small shell, displayed on a shelf.

After one of their trips, I asked them how it had gone. Su said they had done some "intuitive sailing", her favorite way to navigate. They trusted the boat to find its own way without charting a course. They had sailed up the coast, farther north than they had ever ventured before. They found themselves drawn to a remote, unpopulated island, where the indigenous people had held sacred ceremony generations ago. "Did you find any treasures?" I asked. Su smiled with pleasure and left the room. When she came back, her eyes were shining. She held out her hand. Cradled in her palm were three tiny blue beads, luminous, small as grains of barley. Each one had a hole through it as if prepared ever so delicately for an ancient artisan's needle.

THE VIRTUE OF DISCERNMENT

"How on earth did you spot them?" I asked. "We just felt our way," she said, and described how she and Dave had walked the beach for hours, in contemplative vigilance, searching for microscopic holes in the sand. Their quiet discernment had yielded a rare harvest.

When has my intuition alerted me to hidden treasures?

THE VIRTUE OF DISCERNMENT

January 2

How many a sign there is in the heavens and the earth which most men pass by and ignore.

—THE QUR'AN 12

We now are engaged in the cultivation of that spiritual sense, and we shall succeed in proportion as we relax our mental struggle and become receptive to those things which the Spirit of God teaches.

—JOEL S. GOLDSMITH

When in my life have I stopped to discern the meaning of the signs and signals placed in my path?

January 3

Call to me and I will answer you, and will tell you great and hidden things that you have not known.

—JEREMIAH 33

Through the faculty of meditation man attains to eternal life; through it he receives the breath of the Holy Spirit—the bestowal of the Spirit is given in reflection and meditation. The spirit of man is itself informed and strengthened during meditation; through it affairs of which man knew nothing are unfolded before his view.

—'ABDU'L-BAHÁ

*When have I intuited something
I did not know?*

THE VIRTUE OF DISCERNMENT

January 4

It finally feels as if I am finding my way to my own life. In the quietness I now allow myself to take each morning, I realize that this life is mine . . . finally. It has taken me a long time to know that and to unearth it from under all that buried it . . . it is mine and I care deeply about it . . . I am beginning to understand the meaning of the words "to cherish." There is a hush, a sense of waiting . . . as I watch my life unfold itself to me newly each day and beckon me onward to its unfoldment.

—JUDITH DUERK

I cherish quiet time, which allows me to discern the unfoldment of my life.

THE VIRTUE OF DISCERNMENT

January 5

There is no greater blessing a mother can give her daughter than a reliable sense of the veracity of her own intuition. Intuition is handed from parent to child in the simplest ways: "You have good judgment. What do you think lies hidden behind all this?" Rather than defining intuition as some unreasoned faulty quirk, it is defined as truly the soul-voice speaking.

—CLARISSA PINKOLA ESTÉS

How do I encourage myself and others to trust the intuition of our souls?

January 6

... They smelt images from their silver, idols of their own manufacture ... Therefore they will be like morning mist, like the dew that quickly disappears, like the chaff whirled from the threshing floor, like smoke escaping through the window.

—HOSEA 13

Love is yes.

—PETER MCWILLIAMS

What in my life is false, extraneous, to be sifted out and released, and what am I called to say yes to at this time in my life?

THE VIRTUE OF DISCERNMENT

THE PRACTICE OF DISCERNMENT

I am contemplative and vigilant.
I am alert to the signs placed in my path.
I am open to revelation.
I discern the unfoldment of my life in daily
  quiet.
I honor intuition.
I discern my true calling.

*I am thankful for the gift of discernment.
It leads me to the truth.*

THE VIRTUE OF LOVE

January 8

Mark had spent all his adult years in government service. He and Angela had been happily married for forty-two years and had raised three children. They had been saving and planning for years to travel to exotic destinations and were counting the days until retirement so that they could be on their way at last. A few months before he was to retire at sixty-five, Mark learned that he had inoperable cancer and would probably die within six months.

When Mark entered Hospice, I had the privilege of providing spiritual care to him and Angela as they grieved their lost dreams. One morning, a few weeks before his death, a nurse asked me to go to him, saying he was very agitated. As I entered his room, his groans crescendoed to a loud "No!" I pulled a chair close to the bed and looked into his eyes. "What's happening, Mark?" "They're taking everything!" he yelled. "What are they taking?" "Everything. Everything." I sat with him, alert to what was being lost. "Tell me." Calmer, he began to list some of his possessions, odds and ends, saying "No, they can't have that! They can't take that!" When he appeared to come to the end of his list, I asked "What do you want to keep, Mark?" His eyes softened and he relaxed against the pillow. "My wife." He smiled and drifted off to sleep.

If I were going to die tomorrow, what would I really want to keep?

January 9

I loved thy creation, hence I created thee. Wherefore, do thou love Me, that I may name thy name and fill thy soul with the spirit of life.
—BAHÁ'U'LLÁH

Love is an act of faith, and whoever is of little faith is also of little love.
—ERICH FROMM

How often do I have faith in the fact that I am loved?

January 10

If I speak in the tongues of mortals and of angels, but do not have love, I am a noisy gong or a clanging cymbal. And if I have prophetic powers, and understand all mysteries and all knowledge, and if I have all faith, so as to remove mountains, but do not have love, I am nothing. . . . Love is patient; love is kind; love is not envious or boastful or arrogant or rude. It does not insist on its own way; it is not irritable or resentful; it does not rejoice in wrongdoing but rejoices in the truth. It bears all things, believes all things, hopes all things, endures all things. Love never ends . . . And now faith, hope, and love abide, these three; and the greatest of these is love.

—1 CORINTHIANS 13

Who needs my kind and patient love right now?

THE VIRTUE OF LOVE

January 11

Love has nothing to do with what you are expecting to get—only what you are expecting to give—which is everything. What you receive in turn varies. But it really has no connection with what you give. You give because you love and cannot help giving. If you are lucky, you may be loved back. That is delicious, but it does not necessarily happen.

—KATHERINE HEPBURN

I allow myself to love purely, generously,
fully, without worrying about what
I will receive in return.

THE VIRTUE OF LOVE

January 12

Don't do unto others as
you would have them do unto you. They may have
different tastes.

—GEORGE BERNARD SHAW

Love is the child of
freedom, never that of domination.

—ERICH FROMM

How free is my love?

THE VIRTUE OF LOVE

January 13

But if in your fear you would seek only love's peace and love's pleasure, then it is better for you that you cover your nakedness and pass out of love's threshing floor, into the seasonless world where you shall laugh, but not all of your laughter, and weep, but not all of your tears.

—KAHLIL GIBRAN

What work is love calling me to do on myself?

THE VIRTUE OF LOVE

January 14

THE PRACTICE OF LOVE

I know what I really care about.
I allow myself to feel the Creator's love.
I show love in kind and patient ways.
I love others fully, free of expectations.
I love others truly, free of control.
I do the work on myself which love calls me to
   do.

I am thankful for the gift of love.
It is the source of my being.

January 15

Ten First Nations women gathered with me at a lodge for a five-day healing retreat. They shared stories, often things they had never told anyone before, and were received with receptive, loving silence. It took Sharon four days to trust enough to take her turn. She sat in the healing circle, head hanging, her hair a veil to shield her eyes. Some of her teeth had been knocked out and never replaced. She had a shy habit of covering her mouth when she smiled or laughed. Something in the safety and sacredness of the circle gave her courage, for the first time, to tell her story. As she spoke of the abuses of her spirit and body, and how the pain was passed on to her children, the tears of the other women fell with hers. They wept with her silently, holding her in unbroken concentration. When she was finished, she sat limp, spent, but raised her eyes to meet the gaze of each woman in the circle as each one acknowledged her virtues. "I honor you for your courage to survive the abuse." "You were so honest in telling your story." "You had perseverance to live through all this." "I see your purity. You have never lost it."

When the women finished acknowledging her virtues,

THE VIRTUE OF CONFIDENCE

Sharon tossed back her hair, and her face lit up in a wide smile, gaps proudly displayed. A new confidence shone in her eyes. After that, she walked taller. Words of encouragement and compassion to the other women flowed from her. Her heart was open, and she no longer hid her smile.

How does my confidence grow
when I tell my true story?

January 16

For you created my inmost being; you knit me together in my mother's womb. I praise you because I am fearfully and wonderfully made; your works are wonderful, I know that full well. —PSALM 139

I am wonderfully made, gifted and able.
I welcome new possibilities to use
the gifts I was given.

January 17

I created thee rich, why dost thou bring thyself down to poverty? Noble I made thee, wherewith dost thou abase thyself? . . . Turn thy sight unto thyself, that thou mayest find Me standing within thee, mighty, powerful, and self-subsisting. —BAHÁ'U'LLÁH

What do I need to heal in order to know how rich I am?

January 18

Do not throw away your confidence; it brings a great reward.

—HEBREWS 10

If we are not fully ourselves, truly in the present moment, we miss everything.

—THICH NHAT HANH

When do I feel most confident and present?

January 19

We learn wisdom from failure much more than success. We often discover what WILL do, by finding out what will NOT do.

—SAMUEL SMILES

Bless the things which do not turn out right.

—NANCY WOOD

Which of my mistakes have been my best teachers, and what have they taught me?

THE VIRTUE OF CONFIDENCE

January 20

To be trusted is a greater compliment than to be loved.

—GEORGE MACDONALD

Only a person who has faith in himself is able to be faithful to others.

—ERICH FROMM

What am I most confident about in myself?

THE VIRTUE OF CONFIDENCE

January 21

THE PRACTICE OF CONFIDENCE

My confidence grows as I share my story.
I am wonderfully made, and I value my gifts.
I claim the power in my soul.
I am fully myself, present to each moment.
I bless my mistakes and learn from them.
I am faithful to others' confidence in me.

I am thankful for the gift of confidence.
It allows me to be fully and freely myself.

THE VIRTUE OF DETACHMENT

January 22

Maria's husband John was baffled when she first talked of separation, but finally left for three months to give her space. After a disastrous first marriage to an alcoholic who had been very dependent on her, Maria had been swept off her feet by this tall, powerful man who was so caring and dependable. Yet she had suspended so much of her own style, her own thoughts, her own being, in deference to him that she had felt her own self ebbing away. And now she was alone to sift through the longing and the rage, to find the truth about whether she could remain in this marriage or face another divorce. She wept, prayed and grieved her confusion. She stepped back and took a long, detached look at their years together, spreading the photos of their wedding, their trips, the children's birthdays, in chronological order on the living room floor. Gradually, she discerned what needed to change so that she could feel more equal, so that she could love him while remaining free to honor her own boundaries. The day before his homecoming, she felt fragile. "How can I keep from losing myself again?" she prayed. The answer came: "Stand on your own holy ground."

THE VIRTUE OF DETACHMENT

The evening of his return, she found herself wild with childish excitement. She followed him from room to room. She melted in his embrace. She awoke the next morning, sobered by the thought of losing ground. She took her fear into prayer, and, in meditation, saw herself as a child, racing down a path to place her fear at the feet of a Holy Figure. "What do I do now?" she cried. He gazed serenely at her hands. She looked down at her hands and saw that she was holding a small, flat, red wooden valentine heart broken into two halves. "Only give him half," He said. "The other half is Mine." He took it and held it to His heart.

*What boundaries do I need in my
relationships to help me stand
on my own holy ground?*

THE VIRTUE OF DETACHMENT

January 23

Feelings demand to be noticed, and healthy people know what they feel, accept those feelings, and are able to choose how to act in the light of those feelings.

—KATHERINE MARIE DYCKMAN, S.N.J.M. &

L. PATRICK CARROLL, S.J.

When have I been able to accept my feelings without letting them dictate my actions?

THE VIRTUE OF DETACHMENT

January 24

Perform all thy actions with mind concentrated on the Divine, renouncing attachment and looking upon success and failure with an equal eye. Spirituality implies equanimity.
—THE BHAGAVAD GITA 2

*What would give me the detachment
to hold success and failure lightly,
unattached to outcomes?*

THE VIRTUE OF DETACHMENT

January 25

From craving arises sorrow and from lust arises fear. If a man is free from craving, he is free from fear and sorrow.

—THE DHAMMAPADA

You always have the choice to take all things evenly, to hold on to nothing, to receive each irritation as if you had only fifteen minutes to live.

—TOLBERT MCCARROLL

I have the power to detach myself from cravings and irritations, to be alive to what truly matters. It is my choice.

THE VIRTUE OF DETACHMENT

January 26

Detachment is not a cold, hostile withdrawal; a resigned, despairing acceptance of anything life and people throw our way; a robotical walk through life oblivious to, and totally unaffected by people and problems; a Pollyanna-like ignorant bliss; a shirking of our true responsibilities to ourselves and others; a severing of our relationships. Nor is it a removal of our love and concern . . . Ideally, detachment is releasing or detaching from, a person or problem in love . . . Detachment is based on the premise that each person is responsible for himself, that we can't solve problems that aren't ours to solve and that worrying doesn't help . . .

—MELODY BEATTIE

How ready am I to detach from unhealthy enmeshments in my life, to stop taking responsibility for other people and their choices?

January 27

 asked God for strength, that I might achieve.

I was made weak, that I might learn humbly to obey . . .

I asked for health, that I might do great things.

I was given infirmity, that I might do better things . . .

I asked for power, that I might have the praise of men.

I was given weakness, that I might feel the need of God . . .   —ROY CAMPANELLA

*What have I received from the tests
of my life?*

THE VIRTUE OF DETACHMENT

THE PRACTICE OF DETACHMENT

I stand on my own holy ground.
I honor my feelings and freely choose how I will
   act.
I hold success and failure lightly.
I free myself from cravings and irritations.
I am responsible only for myself.
I recognize the blessings in my tests.

I am thankful for detachment.
It gives me a fresh perspective.

THE VIRTUE OF CREATIVITY

January 29

His parents worried so. Albert didn't speak until he was four; didn't read until he was seven. He was a shy, contemplative child. His teachers found him a totally unsatisfactory pupil, apparently incapable of any progress. One teacher described him as "mentally slow, unsociable and adrift forever in his foolish dreams." He was expelled from one school and was refused admittance into another. Because of his father's financial struggles, the family moved often. Albert was a misfit. He encountered anti-Semitic prejudice in every school, and took refuge in his private daydreams.

At fourteen, his life changed dramatically. A young Jewish medical student gave him a book on geometry, which Albert found fascinating. It was as if his mind was awakened after a long sleep. He became a voracious reader of books on philosophy.

He went on to teach at Princeton University, discover the theory of relativity and unlock the secrets of the universe.

*What foolish dreams of mine
call me to creativity?*

January 30

I want to know how God created the world. I am not interested in this or that phenomenon, I want to know God's thoughts, the rest are details.

—ALBERT EINSTEIN

God creates out of nothing. Therefore, until a man is nothing God can make nothing out of him.

—MARTIN LUTHER

When have I felt like nothing, and what was created in me at that time?

THE VIRTUE OF CREATIVITY

January 31

Let us use the different gifts allotted to each of us by God's grace; the gift of inspired utterance, for example, let us use in proportion to our faith; the gift of administration to administer, the gift of teaching to teach, the gift of counseling to counsel.

—ROMANS 12

What are the special gifts allotted to me?

THE VIRTUE OF CREATIVITY

February 1

Writing is easy. All you do is sit staring at the blank sheet of paper until the drops of blood form on your forehead.

—RED SMITH

In order to create, there must be a dynamic force, and what force is more potent than love?

—IGOR STRAVINSKY

My creativity is an act of love. I don't need to make it hard work, only heart work.

THE VIRTUE OF CREATIVITY

February 2

Many instructors of playwriting or fiction advise their students from the earliest planning stages to make an outline or "write it down." This is not necessarily sound. Too early an attempt to snatch at rainbows results in their vanishing entirely. We do better to memorize the colors, integrate the memory, and later try to re-create what it was we saw.

—SOPHY BURNHAM

What inspires my creativity and allows me to capture the full rainbow of my experience?

THE VIRTUE OF CREATIVITY

February 3

Blessed is the soul, which, at the hour of its separation from the body, is sanctified from the vain imaginings of the peoples of the world. Such a soul liveth and moveth in accordance with the Will of its Creator . . . The light which these souls radiate is responsible for the progress of the world and the advancement of its peoples. They are like unto leaven which leaveneth the world of being, and constitute the animating force through which the arts and wonders of the world are made manifest.

—BAHÁ'U'LLÁH

I ask those who guide me to help me access the arts and wonders I am meant to manifest.

THE VIRTUE OF CREATIVITY

THE PRACTICE OF CREATIVITY

I entertain my dreams.
I am a creation of God.
I value my creative gifts.
I work with heart.
I honor my own process of creativity.
I am open to spiritual guidance in accessing my
  creativity.

I am thankful for creativity.
It releases my unique contributions.

THE VIRTUE OF DEVOTION

February 5

When Annie Sullivan arrived at the Keller home, she was fresh from the Perkins Institute for the Blind in Boston and eager to teach. Six-year-old Helen was her first "pupil." An illness had left Helen blind and deaf when she was only nineteen months old. Her parents refused to institutionalize her, and she tyrannized the family with her violent tantrums, unceasing movement and wild, animal-like ways. She destroyed almost everything she touched. At the dinner table, she refused to eat from her own plate. She thrust her hands into other people's plates and smeared the food around and into her mouth. She was never still, except occasionally when she would allow her mother to hold her.

Annie devoted herself to teaching this wild child. Her training ill prepared her to deal with Helen's rages. She realized there could be no real change until she could get Helen away from her loving but over-indulgent family. The tide turned when Annie insisted on taking Helen to a guest cottage on the family property. She intuitively felt that "obedience is the gateway through which knowledge, yes, and love too, enter the mind of the child . . . We had a terrific tussle . . . the struggle lasted for nearly two hours. I never saw such strength and endurance in a child." It was on a day soon after Annie won the battle of wills with the child that Helen suddenly grasped the meaning of the words Annie signed into her hand. Helen Keller recalls that day as the most important day of her life, the day the world opened to her. "The mystery of language was revealed to me. I knew then that "w-a-t-e-r" meant the wonderful cool something that was flowing over my hand. That living word awakened my soul, gave it light, joy, set it free!" Helen graduated from Radcliffe College at twenty-three and became a world renowned author.

To what am I devoted?

THE VIRTUE OF DEVOTION

February 6

The need for devotion to something outside ourselves is even more profound than the need for companionship. If we are not to go to pieces or wither away, we all must have some purpose in life; for no man can live for himself alone.　　　　　—ROSS PARMENTER

What purpose is life calling me to now?

THE VIRTUE OF DEVOTION

February 7

... All effort and exertion put forth by man from the fullness of his heart is worship, if it is prompted by the highest motives and the will to do service to humanity.

—'ABDU'L-BAHÁ

*What would free me to work
from the fullness of my heart?*

THE VIRTUE OF DEVOTION

February 8

When you work for God, not self, it is just as good as meditation. Then work helps your meditation and meditation helps your work. You need the balance. With meditation only, you become lazy. With activity only, the mind becomes worldly and you forget God.

It is when you persistently, selflessly perform every action with love-inspired thoughts of God that He will come to you . . . This is the way of knowing the Lord through activity. When in every action you think of Him before you act, while you are performing the action, and after you have finished it, He will reveal Himself to you. You must work, but let God work through you; this is the best part of devotion. If you are constantly thinking that He is walking through your feet, working through your hands, accomplishing through your will, you will know Him

—PARAMAHANSA YOGANANDA

Today I work with devotion, aware of the Divine presence in all that I do.

THE VIRTUE OF DEVOTION

February 9

Lord, enfold me in the depths of your heart; and there, hold me, refine, purge, and set me on fire, raise me aloft, until my own self knows utter annihilation.

—PIERRE TEILHARD DE CHARDIN

How willing am I to be transformed?

THE VIRTUE OF DEVOTION

February 10

If you build it, he will come.

—WILLIAM P. KINSELLA

The big question is whether you are going to be able to say a hearty yes to your adventure.

—JOSEPH CAMPBELL

What adventure is calling to my heart?

THE VIRTUE OF DEVOTION

February 11

THE PRACTICE OF DEVOTION

I am willing to give my all to what I care about.
I discern the purpose to which life calls me.
I work from the fullness of my heart.
I am aware of the Divine presence in my
   activities.
I surrender myself to my true reality.
I say yes to adventure.

I am thankful for devotion.
It makes me fully alive.

THE VIRTUE OF TRUST

February 12

The other day on retreat, my whole life reconsidered,
I watched a duck flap madly across the water, no height
   gained,
reminding me of me, on my own,
forgetting God.
And then, a gull, merely tilting occasionally for balance,
trusting the current, soared free and powerful
knowing with its body the Source of power.
When will I remember?
The Source of joy and life has held me
in a hollowed hand forever,
and plans no moment without my good in mind.
Now that I am at the end of young and the beginning of
   old,
I crave a life of my own.
My own wisdom
and truth
and knowing
I want to, finally, grow up
or grow in
to hear my own voice so clearly
that all the haunting voices

THE VIRTUE OF TRUST

can no longer suck my power.
I am ready
for new old songs
to have my fruitage joyfully break ground
to dare to stretch my wings,
no flapping necessary,
to find the current
and soar freely into trust
just tilting for balance every now and then.

—EXCERPT FROM *TRUST* BY LINDA KAVELIN POPOV

*What would allow me to trust
freely and fully?*

THE VIRTUE OF TRUST

February 13

Trust in the Lord and He will guide you aright. One who has this trust need fear nothing. He can be at perfect peace and happiness, for he will be guided aright.

—THE MAHAVAGGA 8

Nothing can befall us but what God hath destined for us.

—THE QUR'AN 9

What would change in my life if I released all my limiting fears and trusted in guidance?

February 14

O thou who art turning thy face towards God! Close thine eyes to all things else, and open them to the realm of the All-Glorious. Ask whatsoever thou wishest of Him alone; seek whatsoever thou seekest from Him alone. With a look he granteth a hundred thousand hopes, with a glance He healeth a hundred thousand incurable ills, with a nod He layeth balm on every wound, with a glimpse He freeth the hearts from the shackles of grief. He doeth as He doeth, and what recourse have we? He carrieth out His will, He ordaineth what He pleaseth. Then better for thee to bow down thy head in submission, and put thy trust in the All-Merciful Lord.

—'ABDU'L-BAHÁ

I trust the healing power of prayer.

THE VIRTUE OF TRUST

February 15

As soon as you trust yourself, you will know how to live.

—JOHANN WOLFGANG VON GOETHE

What if woman were to allow herself to trust her own unhappiness and to make life changes—changes that would allow time and place for her to experience her life as it lives itself out slowly, moment by moment? . . . To allow herself to leave behind the jet plane, the express lane, and simply be there, for a moment, present to her life? . . . What if she trusted her anger, her irritation, her illness, even her depression, as signs that her own life was calling to her?

—JUDITH DUERK

I trust the signals which come from my spirit, my emotions and my body. I am willing to listen to the message.

THE VIRTUE OF TRUST

February 16

The wise student hears of the Tao and practices it diligently. The average student hears of the Tao and gives it thought now and again. The foolish student hears of the Tao and laughs aloud. If there were no laughter, the Tao would not be what it is. Hence it is said:

The bright path seems dim;
Going forward seems like retreat;
The easy way seems hard;
The highest Virtue seems empty;
Great purity seems sullied;
A wealth of Virtue seems inadequate;
The strength of Virtue seems frail;
Real Virtue seems unreal;
The perfect square has no corners;
Great talents ripen late;
The highest notes are hard to hear . . .
The Tao alone nourishes and brings everything to fulfillment.

—TAO TE CHING (THE WAY AND ITS POWER)

In my heart of hearts, I trust the true wealth of the spiritual path. I am a willing student.

THE VIRTUE OF TRUST

February 17

...Those who wait for the Lord shall renew their strength, they shall mount up with wings like eagles, they shall run and not be weary, they shall walk and not faint.

—ISAIAH 40

How can I learn to trust my Creator completely?

THE VIRTUE OF TRUST

February 18

THE PRACTICE OF TRUST

I trust the seasons of my life.

I trust my destiny.

I trust the power of prayer.

I trust the wisdom of my own experience.

I trust that the spiritual path leads to
fulfillment.

I am uplifted by trust in my Creator.

*I am thankful for the gift of trust.
It renews my strength.*

THE VIRTUE OF PURITY

February 19

I had a pivotal experience in meditation one day with the virtue of purity. It was a time when I was quite emotionally sunk, spiritually bogged down. I began to meditate and saw myself sitting, cross-legged, shoulders slumped, at the edge of a small, crystal clear pool on a high bluff. I was drawn to immerse myself in this pool, which I sensed was a place of purification, yet I just sat there, immobilized. I was wearing a dirty, clodden cloak which weighed heavily on my shoulders. Suddenly, I felt the cloak being lifted gently from behind. The Angel of Purity flung the cloak over a waterfall which flowed into another pool far below. As the cloak fell, it turned into leaves which drifted apart on the surface of the water. For me, this vision meant it was time to purify myself of old pain which was weighing me down needlessly; that, with help from the spiritual realm, this was possible. This vision remained with me for days, during which I felt lighter, freer. Joy kept bubbling up to the surface of my awareness.

*What needless pain do I carry
that I am called to release?*

February 20

The man who wisely controls his senses as a good driver controls his horses, and who is free from lower passions and pride, is admired even by the gods; he is calm like the earth that endures; he is steady like a column that is firm; he is pure like a lake that is clear . . . In the light of his vision he has found his freedom: his thoughts are peace, his words are peace and his work is peace.

—THE DHAMMAPADA 7

What are the desires that control me and what are the true desires of my heart?

THE VIRTUE OF PURITY

February 21

... Christ has addressed the world, saying, "Except ye be converted, and become as little children, ye shall not enter into the kingdom of heaven"—that is, men must become pure in heart to know God ... The hearts of all children are of the utmost purity. They are mirrors on which no dust has fallen ... But this purity is on account of weakness and innocence, not on account of any strength and testing ... whereas the man becomes pure through his strength ... his heart becomes purified, his spirit enlightened, his soul is sensitized and tender—all through his great strength. This is the difference between the perfect man and the child. Both have the underlying qualities of simplicity and sincerity—the child through the power of weakness and the man through the power of strength.

—'ABDU'L-BAHÁ

What tests in my life have refined me and brought me back to simplicity?

THE VIRTUE OF PURITY

February 22

s a man thinketh in his heart, so is he. —PROVERBS 23

leanse thou the rheum from out thine head and breathe the breath of God instead. —JALALU'D-DIN RUMI

What congests my thinking? What do I need to cleanse, to make room for inspiration?

THE VIRTUE OF PURITY

February 23

Puritanism is the haunting fear that someone, somewhere, may be happy.

—H. L. MENCKEN

We want cookie!

—THE COOKIE MONSTER

How can I make peace between the puritan in me and the desires of my pure nature?

February 24

Your soul is often-
times a battlefield, upon which your reason and
your judgment wage war against your passion and
your appetite. Would that I could be the peace-
maker in your soul, that I might turn the discord
and the rivalry of your elements into oneness and
melody.

But how shall I, unless you yourselves be also
the peacemakers, nay, the lovers of all your elements?   —KHALIL GIBRAN

*What are the elements in me that need
to be lovingly integrated?*

THE VIRTUE OF PURITY

February 25

THE PRACTICE OF PURITY

I release needless pain.
I heal my addictive desires.
I reclaim my innocence.
I clear my mind to make room for inspiration.
I distinguish between purity and puritanism.
I love and accept all my elements.

I am thankful for the gift of purity.
It brings clarity to my soul.

THE VIRTUE OF HUMILITY

February 26

By the third day of the virtues workshop, the trust in the group had deepened amazingly. We were all so different—clergy, day-care workers, therapists; African-American, Asian, white; Jewish, Siddha Yoga, Bahá'í, Catholic, Quaker, Methodist, agnostic. A quiet reverence came over us as each one spoke of a sacred moment. One person spoke of a moment of pristine oneness while he ran at dawn; another of a sense of being mysteriously comforted in her grief; others related hearing God's voice. The last to speak was a minister, a gentle man in his sixties. He stood up slowly and faced the hushed circle. There was a tremor in his voice. "I have never been able to pray like some of you. I have tried, many times. The connection just doesn't happen." He paused to regain his composure. "All I get are hunches." He went on. "I went to the hospital to visit someone and found she had checked out. I started to leave but something, some nudge, told me to enter another room. The person in that room needed comforting." "That's all I get— hunches." His humility filled the room.

What simple gift deserves my recognition?

THE VIRTUE OF HUMILITY

February 27

With what shall I come before the Lord, and bow myself before God on high? ... He has told you, O mortal, what is good: and what does the Lord require of you but to do justice, and to love kindness, and to walk humbly with your God?　　　　　—MICAH 6

I am humble before the power of spirit, alert for opportunities to be just and kind.

THE VIRTUE OF HUMILITY

February 28

The life which is not examined is not worth living.   —PLATO

See what you lack and not what you have, for that is the quickest path to humility.   —THE CLOUD OF UNKNOWING

When I examine myself with humility, what virtues am I called upon to develop?

February 29

 lift up my eyes to the
hills—
    from where will my help come?
    My help comes from the lord,
    who made heaven and earth.

—PSALM 121

h I get by with a little
help from my friends.   —PAUL MCCARTNEY

How often do I have the humility
to ask for help?

THE VIRTUE OF HUMILITY

March 1

Humility is not an abstract thing. Neither is it a melodramatic self-abasement which you inflict on others. Humility is washing out the bathtub, making your own bed, getting your own tea. Stop the game of getting out of menial tasks. Bend. Do not expect others to wait on you. Go the other way. Do things for others.

It is much easier for you to serve the lepers in the South Seas than to clean the ring out of the bathtub. When you serve the lepers you prove to yourself that you are special. When you wash the bathtub you learn that you have a common connection with every other person. No one is better than anyone else, and no one really believes that.

—TOLBERT MCCARROL

Today I feel the common connection, and seek simple ways to serve others.

March 2

He sat down, called the twelve, and said to them, "Whoever wants to be first must be last of all and servant of all."

—MARK 9

We come nearest to the great when we are great in humility.

—RABINDRANATH TAGORE

When do I place myself over others, pushing to be first, and when am I content to be a true servant?

THE VIRTUE OF HUMILITY

March 3

Man is not intended to see through the eyes of another, hear through another's ears nor comprehend with another's brain. Each human creature has individual endowment, power and responsibility in the creative plan of God.
—'ABDU'L-BAHÁ

For the most part, I do the thing which my own nature prompts me to do. It is embarrassing to earn so much respect and love for it.
—ALBERT EINSTEIN

What are the powers in my own nature
for which am I most thankful?

THE VIRTUE OF HUMILITY

March 4

THE PRACTICE OF HUMILITY

I recognize my simple gifts.
I walk humbly with my God, seeking ways to be
  just and kind.
I am willing to keep improving.
I ask for help when I need it.
I serve others.
I am aware of my pride.
I am humbled by my powers.

I am thankful for the gift of humility.
It helps me to see myself honestly.

THE VIRTUE OF COMPASSION

March 5

She stood before the microphone, leaning on her cane, her face pale and lovely. In a gentle voice, she spoke of her near death experience at age sixteen. Her throat had swollen shut, and she was pronounced dead on arrival at the hospital. After forty-five minutes, her physician finally succeeded in resuscitating her.

While she was not breathing, she watched her body until gradually she experienced a transcendence to another world. She was drawn to a light and found herself in the presence of a Being who emanated profound love and tenderness. Through sharing His perception, she saw the panorama of her life, instantly assessing the value of each moment. She had been an accomplished student, but the achievements she considered to be important were mere pin-pricks of light. Then she saw a moment when she had reached out to a disabled child at camp, brought him a drink of water and soothed his feelings of rejection. This one act of compassion shone out in a blaze of glory.

When have I valued simple acts of compassion in their true light?

March 6

Who is incapable of hatred towards any being, who is kind and compassionate, free from selfishness . . . such a devotee of Mine is My beloved.

—THE BHAGAVAD GITA 12

Finally, all of you, be of one mind, sympathetic, loving toward one another, compassionate, humble. Do not return evil for evil, or insult for insult; but on the contrary, a blessing, because to this you were called, that you might inherit a blessing.

—PETER 3

What resentments and negativities do I need to free myself from in order to access my compassion?

THE VIRTUE OF COMPASSION

March 7

se a minute
feel some sorrow
for the folks
who think tomorrow
is a place that they
can call up
on the phone.
Take a month
and show some kindness
for the folks
who thought that blindness
was an illness that
affected eyes alone.

—EXCERPT FROM *TAKE TIME OUT*

BY MAYA ANGELOU

*What time shall I take and what can I do to
reach out in compassion to those that need it?*

March 8

Please call me by my true names; so I can hear all my cries and laughs at once, so I can see that my joy and pain are one.

—THICH NHAT HANH

To "listen" another's soul into a condition of disclosure and discovery may be almost the greatest service that any human being ever performs for another.

—DOUGLAS STEEN

When have I given someone the gift of hearing their own joy and pain?

March 9

As one whom his mother comforteth, so will I comfort you.

—ISAIAH 40

He will never deal unjustly with anyone, neither will He task a soul beyond its power. He, verily, is the Compassionate, the All-Merciful.

—BAHÁ'U'LLÁH

What if I believed that everything that happens is for my good?

March 10

llowing expression to the child of the past that experienced the trauma and developing compassion, rather than contempt for that child, is the essence of the grief work process.

—JANE MIDDLETON-MOZ & LORIE DWINELL

If your compassion does not include yourself, it is incomplete.

—JACK KORNFIELD

How compassionate am I when I need to grieve? How do I show compassion to myself?

THE VIRTUE OF COMPASSION

March 11

THE PRACTICE OF COMPASSION

I value acts of compassion in their true light.
I release negativity that shuts others out.
I take time to reach out to those who need help.
I care for others by listening deeply.
I see the compassion in all that happens to me.
I have compassion for myself.

*I am thankful for the gift of compassion.
It stirs my heart.*

March 12

The first time I saw Jim was at an outdoor market. An attendant was wheeling him by. Our eyes met, and I smiled. He flashed back a crooked grin. Six months later, I was in the forward lounge of a large ferry and saw him again, sitting in his wheelchair. I stopped and looked into his eyes.

"Do I know you?" he asked, his speech slurred, his hands waving like limp flags.

"Yes. We met at the craft market," I replied.

"Oh, yeah."

"Are you coming or going?"

"Oh, I'm coming back from vegetable camp," he replied.

"What are you, a carrot?"

"No, a squash!" The sound of our laughter turned heads. His laugh was loud, a drawing in of breath which sounded like a donkey braying. I sat down next to him. Between jokes, he told me his story. He had a premonition in his teens that he was going to die. Shortly after that he was in a serious car accident that left him a paraplegic. "But I never expected this," he said. "This is harder."

THE VIRTUE OF ACCEPTANCE

As the ferry was pulling into dock, I asked him what it was that gave him such good humor. "I'm lucky," he said. "What else could happen to me?"

"Well, your hair could fall out." This time he roared with laughter. The attendant came running and started to wheel him away.

"Wait!" said Jim.

He took my hand somehow between his and brought it to his lips.

*What test in my life have I accepted
with grace and humor?*

March 13

In Buddhism, the word "suchness" is used to mean "the essence or particular characteristics of a thing or person, its true nature." Each person has his or her suchness. If we want to live in peace and happiness with a person, we have to see the suchness of that person. Once we see it, we understand him or her, and there will be no trouble. We can live peacefully and happily together.

—THICH NHAT HANH

What would allow me to be totally accepting of the "suchness" of those I care for?

March 14

Would ye apprehend with what wonders of My munificence and bounty I have willed to entrust your souls, ye would, of a truth, rid yourselves of attachment to all created things, and would gain a true knowledge of your own selves—a knowledge which is the same as the comprehension of Mine own being. Ye would find yourselves independent of all else but Me, and would perceive, with your inner and outer eye . . . the seas of My loving-kindness and bounty moving within you.

—BAHÁ'U'LLÁH

What would free me to accept myself,
my true Self?

March 15

Let the words of my mouth, and the meditation of my heart, be acceptable in thy sight, O Lord, my strength, and my redeemer.

—PSALM 19

Give me grace ever to desire and to will what is most acceptable to thee and most pleasing in thy sight.

—THOMAS À KEMPIS

*How aligned is my will
with what God wills for me?*

THE VIRTUE OF ACCEPTANCE

March 16

If children live with criticism,
   they learn to condemn . . .
   If children live with tolerance,
   they learn to be patient.
   If children live with encouragement,
   they learn to be confident.
   If children live with praise,
   they learn to appreciate.
   If children live with approval,
   they learn to like themselves.

—EXCERPT FROM *CHILDREN LEARN WHAT THEY LIVE*
                              BY DOROTHY NOLTE

Have I learned to like myself?

March 17

God grant me the serenity to accept the things I cannot change, the courage to change the things I can, and the wisdom to know the difference.

—REINHART NIEBUHR

What in my life do I most need to accept?

THE VIRTUE OF ACCEPTANCE

March 18

THE PRACTICE OF ACCEPTANCE

I accept my tests with humor and grace.
I accept my intimates as they are.
I accept myself as a wondrous creation.
I seek Divine acceptance.
I like myself.
I accept those things I cannot change.

I am thankful for acceptance.
It brings me serenity.

THE VIRTUE OF GRACE

March 19

Grace can be gentle like water
its power hidden by the soft flowing
yet wearing away rock imperturbably.
No one watching can tell
how its cutting force is wielded.
The trick is not to block the flow,
with impediments silted by self-deprecation,
the accumulated muck
and rancid leaves of shame
to clog the way.
Grace flows only where there is an opening.
It pools at obstacles,
waits with infinite patience,
never trespasses where it
is not free to go.
Yet, a single sorrow healed
and Grace floods through in an instant.

—*GRACE* BY LINDA KAVELIN POPOV

*What obstacles in me block the flow
of grace in my life?*

THE VIRTUE OF GRACE

March 20

When one is going through major change, a new job, a new life, there is a lot of fear of the unknowns. It's like kayaking on white water. You're paddling. You're upright. There's speed, beauty, and a sense of grace. And at any moment, you could turn a corner, lose your balance and turn over. Meanwhile, all you do is keep paddling and remain upright.

—JOHN KAVELIN

The will of God will never take you where the grace of God cannot sustain you.

—ANONYMOUS

When has a sense of grace
brought me over troubled waters?

March 21

... We put it out to bid, and it came in massively over budget. I felt terrible, crippling shame. I was absolutely alone. I was co-ordinator of the project and I had failed ...

Finding myself revealed in the concrete details of contracting and struggling with new learning, uncertainties, and mistakes as we worked through the nasty surprise that wasn't supposed to happen, I had fallen into a stance of functional atheism. I don't think I'm exaggerating. When I say, "I am responsible here, success or failure; ultimately it's mine," I carry responsibility without grace. I am attempting a spiritual practice without God.

—DONALD SCHELL, S. J.

When am I a functional atheist, trying to do it all myself, forgetting about grace?

March 22

Have no desires in the world. Let God's Grace suffice . . . It is a mistake to believe that human desire and prayer will bring God to your side. There must be a rising in consciousness until His presence is attained—and there rest. Here truly is a perennial rest from care, concern, doubt and fear.

—JOEL S. GOLDSMITH

At the heart of God is a table set for everyone, and God is yearning to have them all home again.   —JAMES M. KEEGAN, S. J.

*When have I allowed myself to be
nurtured by grace?*

March 23

et each one of God's loved ones centre his attention on this: to be the Lord's mercy to man; to be the Lord's grace. Let him do some good to every person whose path he crosseth, and be of some benefit to him . . . In this way, the light of divine guidance will shine forth, and the blessings of God will cradle all mankind. . . . —'ABDU'L-BAHÁ

In what ways have I been the Lord's grace to others? To what is grace calling me now?

March 24

or he shall give his
angels charge over thee, to keep thee in all thy ways.

—PSALM 91

here can I go from
your spirit?
Or where can I flee from your presence? . . .
If I take the wings of the morning
and settle at the farthest limits of the sea
even there your hand shall lead me,
and your right hand shall hold me fast.

—PSALM 139

No matter what is happening in my life,
Spirit is present, watching over me,
leading me, holding my hand.

March 25

THE PRACTICE OF GRACE

I heal what blocks me from the flow of Grace.
I trust Grace to carry me through times of
  change.
I rely on Grace to help me when I am in trouble.
I am free of worry.
I share Grace by serving others.
I am aware of Grace watching over me always.

I am thankful for the gift of grace.
It flows through my life.

THE VIRTUE OF RESPONSIBILITY

March 26

One evening the telephone rang. Before I could finish saying "Hello," my son Craig, breathless with excitement, said "Mom, you won't believe what just happened. It was awesome!" He and a friend had had a sailing accident. The boat had capsized far from shore in a remote part of a deep lake. No other boats were around. The mast of the boat had lodged in the bottom of the lake. They had no life preservers (I held my tongue). Craig swam around the boat several times, trying to right it, but it wouldn't budge. He kept shouting at his friend to help, but the boy couldn't reach high enough to grab the center board. Craig knew he would have to descend into the murk to somehow free the mast. And then he saw them—leaches on the upturned bottom of the boat. I shivered, remembering his fear of little sucking creatures which dated back to a time when, on a rubber raft at age six, he was stung badly by a school of jellyfish before we could get to him.

It took him three tries. The first time, he swam down into the murky darkness, he confirmed that the mast was stuck. He swam up for air, went down again and with great effort, freed the mast and began to right the boat. By the time he got up to the surface it was going back under. "Grab the center board!" he shouted to his friend, who was still in shock. It took one more try, this time with Craig swimming madly to the other side to put all his weight on the board. He pulled his friend up into the boat, and they made it back. He was utterly exhilarated. "I did it, Mom! Yesss!" I smiled into the phone basking with him in the victory, and honored him for his courage and responsibility before issuing a brief sound bite about the value and necessity of wearing life preservers.

To what challenges in my life have I been truly able to respond?

March 27

. . . Until a woman becomes interested in what is real and true in her particular life, until she wants personally to "taste and know how good the Lord is," she can pray and practice and perform rituals with great sincerity and discipline without ever coming to the reality beneath the forms . . . But once we are willing to embody the sacred in our lives, our maturing can proceed. We can say in effect, "I already know I'm a child of God. The question is, how can I become an adult of God?"

—SHERRY RUTH ANDERSON & PATRICIA HOPKINS
(INCLUDING PARAPHRASE OF MARJORY ZOET BANKSON)

When have I experienced a sense of true spiritual maturity?

THE VIRTUE OF RESPONSIBILITY

March 28

e who finds the right
path does so for himself; and he who goes astray
does so to his own loss; and no one who carries a
burden bears another's load.

—THE QUR'AN 17

o one purifies an-
other.
    Never neglect your work
    For another's,
    However great his need.
    Your work is to discover your work
    And then with all your heart
    To give yourself to it.

—THE DHAMMAPADA 12

*When do I neglect my own personal work by
trying to do someone else's?*

THE VIRTUE OF RESPONSIBILITY

March 29

Thou didst do that which was grievous unto me; for thou didst forsake thy ministry . . . no excuse for thee, my son. Thou shouldst have tended to the ministry wherewith thou wast entrusted.

—BOOK OF MORMON, ALMA 39

My life is an influence on every life mine touches. Whether I realize it or not, I am responsible and accountable for that influence.
—RON BARON

How have I forsaken responsibility, and when have I been responsive to the opportunity to minister to others?

THE VIRTUE OF RESPONSIBILITY

March 30

Bring thyself to account each day ere thou art summoned to a reckoning; for death, unheralded, shall come upon thee and thou shalt be called to give account for thy deeds.

—BAHÁ'U'LLÁH

I'd like to make a motion that we face reality.

—BOB NEWHART SHOW

Each day I take the time to reflect on my choices. I face the reality of my victories as well as my mistakes. Seeing the positives helps me to clean up the negatives.

THE VIRTUE OF RESPONSIBILITY

March 31

When we talk about taking responsibility for our lives, we must clarify what we mean by responsibility. The addictive meaning of the word responsibility means accountability and blame . . . Unfortunately, this attitude puts us in the position of being a victim and robbing us of our power.

It is only when we accept that we do have choices, and we exercise those choices, that we can reclaim our lives. Inherent in this reclaiming process is owning the choices we have made (all of them!) and moving on. Thus we are not blaming ourselves for our lives; we are claiming them and owning them so we can take our next steps.

—ANNE WILSON SCHAEF

How free am I to take responsibility for my choices, without shaming or blaming myself?

THE VIRTUE OF RESPONSIBILITY

April 1

THE PRACTICE OF RESPONSIBILITY

I am able to respond to life's challenges.
I honor the truth of my own experience.
I do my own spiritual work.
I am aware of my ability to make a difference.
I am accountable for my victories and my
  mistakes.
Taking responsibility frees me from shame and
  blame.

I am thankful for responsibility.
It gives me the freedom to choose.

THE VIRTUE OF RESPECT

April 2

In the women's circle, Marcella spoke shyly, "I guess it's my turn." She was a tiny woman, waiflike, innocent. As she told of her abusive marriage, her sweet, whispery voice did little to conceal her rage. She described her husband's rude, sarcastic, condescending attitude. She, in turn, shut him out by refusing to speak to him or show him affection, her silent contempt equally effective in building a wall between them. When she finished her story, she was invited to stand. The women stood close as she chanted "I expect respect at all times." At first a whisper, a whine, a child begging. Then the other voices joined, and it became a demand, a roar, and Marcella was belting it out: "I expect respect at all times!" tears coursing down her face.

When she returned home from the retreat, her husband sat at the kitchen table, casually stirring his coffee. She noticed the tightness in his shoulders and the fear in his eyes. "Well?" he asked. "It was great," she said. She walked over and touched his shoulder. "We have a lot to talk about."

How can I raise the level of respect
in my relationships?

THE VIRTUE OF RESPECT

April 3

A man is not an elder because his head is grey; his age may be ripe, but he is called "Old in vain." He in whom truth, virtue, gentleness, self-control, moderation, he who is steadfast and free from impurity, is rightly called an elder . . . is called respectable.

—THE DHAMMAPADA

What virtues in me are respectable, and what virtues do I need to develop?

April 4

There is a longing among all people and creatures to have a sense of purpose and worth. To satisfy that common longing in all of us we must respect each other.

In the olden times man and creature walked as friends who carried the beauty of the land in their hearts. Now each one of us is needed to make sure the salmon can find a place to spawn and the bear cub a tree to climb.

There is little time left and much effort needed!

—CHIEF DAN GEORGE

What daily practices would express my respect for the gifts of the earth? How can I be a respectful consumer every day?

THE VIRTUE OF RESPECT

April 5

ho cannot love herself
cannot love anybody
   who is ashamed of her body is ashamed of all
life . . .
   who cannot respect the gifts given even before
birth
   can never respect anything fully.

—ANNE CAMERON

e do not possess our
homes, our children, or even our own body. They
are given to us for a short while to treat with care
and respect.

—JACK KORNFIELD

How respectfully do I care for my body?

April 6

ften we hear the question: How do you treat people? A far more important question is: How do you treat ideas?

Treat them tenderly.
They can be killed quickly.
Treat them gently . . .
They can be bruised in infancy.
Treat them respectfully . . .
They could be the most valuable thing
that ever came into your life.
. . . Treat them responsibly!
Respond! Act! Do something with them!

—ROBERT SCHULLER

What ideas have caught my attention lately?
What actions would show respect
for their value?

THE VIRTUE OF RESPECT

April 7

 Great Spirit, whose
voice I hear in the winds
and whose breath gives life to all the world,
hear me.
I am small and weak.
I need your strength and wisdom.
Let me walk in beauty
and let my eyes ever behold the red and purple
sunset.
Make my hands respect the things you have
made
and my ears grow sharp to hear your voice . . .
Make me always ready
to come to you with clean hands and straight
eyes.
So when life fades as the fading sunset
my spirit may come to you without shame.

—NATIVE AMERICAN TRADITION

Creator, hear my prayer.
Help me to respect the sacredness of life.

THE VIRTUE OF RESPECT

April 8

THE PRACTICE OF RESPECT

I expect respect at all times.
I live in a way that is worthy of respect.
I do my part to respect the earth.
I respect the gifts I have been given, including
  my body.
I act on the ideas which come to me.
I respect the sacredness of life.

I am thankful for the gift of respect.
It helps me to handle life with care.

THE VIRTUE OF REVERENCE

April 9

What was it about you that touched me so?
I crept closer, hardly daring to breathe
lest you notice and choose to leave.
Head submerged, you came up snorting,
chewing, imperturbable.

Something about your huge grace,
earth-colored, dripping coat,
your willing communion.
I loved you for pretending not to notice me
standing there on the shore, a few breaths away.
And then the squawking tourists screeched to a halt
And disturbed our mutual reverie.

What is it about you that brings an ache to my heart?
An immediacy in your way of life
so unlike my own at the other end of the Alaska Highway
where I am enslaved by ringing phones,
commanded by blinking computer screens.

The piles of paper claim such self-importance
that I begin to forget the real

THE VIRTUE OF REVERENCE

and lose myself in demands
which expand to fill the time
I once found
slow as a beating heart
clear as the mountain lake
where you and I met
that summer day.

—*REVERENCE* BY LINDA KAVELIN POPOV

*What has been one of my
most sacred moments?*

April 10

Man is most truly himself . . . not when he toils but when he adores.

—VIDA P. SCUDDER

Affirmation of life is the spiritual act by which man ceases to live unreflectively and begins to devote himself to his life with reverence in order to raise it to its true value. To affirm life is to deepen, to make more inward, and to exalt the will to live.

—ALBERT SCHWEITZER

What simple, life-affirming practices help me to deepen my reverence?

April 11

f I worship thee for fear of hell, then burn me in hell.

And if I worship thee for hope of heaven, exclude me thence.

But if I worship thee for thine own sake, withhold not from me thine eternal beauty.

—RABIA THE MYSTIC

Today, I walk in reverence. I have no need to lust after outcomes. I feel unconditional appreciation for the Source of life.

THE VIRTUE OF REVERENCE

April 12

I am going to venture that the man who sat on the ground in his tepee meditating on life and its meaning, accepting the kinship of all creatures, and acknowledging unity with the universe of things was infusing into his being the true essence of civilization.

—LUTHER STANDING BEAR

When in my life have I felt a sense of oneness?

April 13

. . . The voice of the Great Spirit is heard in the twittering of birds, the rippling of mighty waters, and the sweet breathing of flowers. If this is Paganism, then at present, at least, I am a Pagan.

—GERTRUDE SIMMONS BONNIN

When am I most aware of the presence of Spirit?

April 14

I am made whole again—my self is given back to me—in solitude and silence.

—ANTHONY DE MELLO

Meditation and action—
He who knows these two together,
. . . gains immortality.

—THE UPANISHADS

What would allow me to balance meditation
and activity, to create the sacred time
to find myself?

April 15

THE PRACTICE OF REVERENCE

I expose myself to beauty.

I have a life-affirming attitude.

I have unconditional appreciation for the
Source of life.

I feel a kinship with all beings.

I am in the presence of Spirit.

I meditate in silence, which makes me whole
again.

I am thankful for the gift of reverence.
It makes my life sacred.

THE VIRTUE OF TRUTHFULNESS

April 16

One of the gifts in my life is my relationship with Judi, who is both friend and spiritual co-director. In spiritual direction, we share our experiences of prayer, our sleeping and waking dreams, our struggles and challenges. We love to challenge each other with perfectly honed questions which help the other to get to her deepest truth. Our relationship is enriched by the fact that we are of different faiths. She is a Roman Catholic nun. I am a Bahá'í.

During one spiritual direction session, I shared with Judi an experience in meditation which surprised me. I had gone into meditation one morning, intending to walk down my "regular" path to my inner sacred place. Instead, I felt a crunch under my shoes, looked down and noticed I was on a gravel path leading to the shrine of the founder of my faith. At first, I pulled back, feeling unworthy, but was drawn magnetically toward the entrance. I went in and placed my head on the threshold. Suddenly, I felt a hand slip under my face and the other hand stroking my hair. I stayed there for a long time. I sighed after telling Judi of this meditation, "For the first time in my life I am aware that I am totally loved, that I am really OK." I described to her the peace I felt in my own skin since this meditation occurred. "You know, Jude, I feel like I'm just now growing up. It's pretty embarrassing at this age." Judi said, "Well, we've lived a half century from our persona. Now it's time to live from our essence."

What illusion would I need to give up,
to live from my essence?

THE VIRTUE OF TRUTHFULNESS

April 17

e shall know the truth,
and the truth shall make you free.

—JOHN 8

his   above   all—to
thine own self be true,
    And it must follow, as the night the day,
    Thou canst not then be false to any man.

—WILLIAM SHAKESPEARE

*What would free me to face the truth about
the issues in my life?*

April 18

ruth is within our-
selves.
There is an inmost centre in us all,
Where the Truth abides in fullness; and to know
Rather consists in opening out a way
Whence the imprisoned splendour may escape
Than in effecting entry for a light
Supposed to be without.

—ROBERT BROWNING

I look within and open myself to Truth.

THE VIRTUE OF TRUTHFULNESS

April 19

Then have done with falsehood and speak the truth to each other, for we belong to one another as parts of one body.

—EPHESIANS 4

Tell the truth. Do it now.

—WERNER ERHARDT

What prevents me from being completely truthful with others, and what would allow me to do it?

April 20

Truthfulness is the foundation of all human virtues. Without truthfulness progress and success, in all the worlds of God, are impossible for any soul. When this holy attribute is established in man, all the divine qualities will also be acquired.
—'ABDU'L-BAHÁ

Truth is the secret of eloquence and of virtue, the basis of moral authority; it is the highest summit of art and life.
—H. F. AMIEL

I stand on a foundation of truth, and it supports all my other virtues.

April 21

It always comes back to the same necessity: go deep enough and there is a bedrock of truth, however hard.

—MAY SARTON

If a man does not keep pace with his companions, perhaps it is because he hears a different drummer. Let him step to the music which he hears, however measured or far away.

—HENRY DAVID THOREAU

What is my deepest truth
at this time in my life?

THE VIRTUE OF TRUTHFULNESS

April 22

THE PRACTICE OF TRUTHFULNESS

I live from my deepest truth.
I tell myself the truth about the issues in my life.
I seek the truth within my spirit.
I tell the truth to others, aware that we are one.
I stand on a foundation of truthfulness.
I am ready to discern what is real and true in my
  life.

I am thankful for the gift of truthfulness.
It sets me free.

THE VIRTUE OF GENEROSITY

April 23

There are times when the Angels of Virtue come un-bidden. A business associate and I had parted after a long, close relationship. It was a painful time. She asked me to come and talk with her about settling with one another. As I was getting into the car, I thought, "I need the virtue of Justice," but suddenly what popped into my awareness was a vision of Generosity, rosy-cheeked and plump, with an uncanny resemblance to Cinderella's fairy godmother. She held out her dirndl skirt, suggesting amplitude. She grinned and waved her arm in a circular gesture which said clearly, "There is plenty of room for your feelings and hers, for her point of view and yours."

When I arrived, the tension in the air fairly crackled. We sat on either end of the couch. I said, "Let's each share our perceptions of what has happened. Please go first, if you like," and moved my arm as Generosity had. Before I left, there was an embrace of mutual acceptance. Justice had indeed been served, but only because generosity had made it possible.

How can I practice generosity in giving more space for the feelings and views of others?

April 24

God will compensate
each one out of His abundance.

—THE QUR'AN 4

And I will restore to you
the years that the locust hath eaten . . .

—JOEL 2

When in my life has loss led to abundance?

THE VIRTUE OF GENEROSITY

April 25

Consider this: whoever sows sparingly will also reap sparingly, and whoever sows bountifully will also reap bountifully. Each must do as already determined, without sadness or compulsion, for God loves a cheerful giver.

—CORINTHIANS 9

One of the marks of true genius is a quality of abundance. A rich, rollicking abundance, enough to give indigestion to ordinary people.

—CATHERINE DRINKER BOWEN

*What allows me to go beyond scarcity,
to give abundantly and cheerfully?*

April 26

The poor in your midst are My trust; guard ye My trust, and be not intent only on your own ease. . . .

To give and to be generous are attributes of Mine; well is it with him that adorneth himself with My virtues. —BAHÁ'U'LLÁH

A man of humanity is one who, in seeking to establish himself, finds a foothold for others and who, desiring attainment for himself, helps others to attain.

—CONFUCIUS

Today I seek ways to be generous to others, aware that they are a trust from God.

April 27

The gift which is given without thought of recompense, in the belief that it ought to be made, in a fit place, at an opportune time and to a deserving person—such a gift is Pure.

That which is given for the sake of the results it will produce, or with the hope of recompense, or grudgingly—that may truly be said to be an outcome of Passion.

—THE BHAGAVAD GITA 17

When I give to others,
what are my true motives?

April 28

Ask and it will be given you; search and you will find; knock and the door will be opened for you. —MATTHEW 7

To those leaning on the sustaining infinite, today is big with blessings. —MARY BAKER EDDY

I dare to ask for my heart's desire.
I am willing to receive.

THE VIRTUE OF GENEROSITY

April 29

THE PRACTICE OF GENEROSITY

I give plenty of space for the feelings and views
  of others.
I am aware of the abundance in my life.
I am a cheerful giver.
I am generous to those in need.
I give without strings attached.
I am receptive to blessings.

I am thankful for generosity.
It helps me to give and receive.

April 30

John was readmitted to Hospice a few days before he was expected to die. When I entered the dim, quiet room, he smiled weakly and reached out his hand. "What kind of a day are you having, John?" I asked. He was getting so thin, hardly there anymore, this once energetic, powerful presence. "Horrible," he whispered. I focused my attention, allowing time for him to go on. As the silence continued, I spoke again, "How is it horrible?"

"I can't move. I can't think. I can't eat. I can't talk. I can't drink. I can't go. I can't breathe . . . " The litany went on for some time. He finally stopped and I breathed with him, matching his pace.

When I sensed it was time for me to go, I asked "What was helpful about talking to me, John?"

He responded in a clear voice and smiled one of his old, vibrant smiles, and said, "Oh, I love you more than anyone on earth."

I was taken aback and quickly looked around, hopeful than none of John's relatives had returned and overheard. Yet, I knew this was what he needed to say.

"What do you love, John?"

"With you, I can say what I need to say, do what I

need to do, feel what I need to feel, cry when I need to cry . . . "

His eyes were radiant. He somehow managed to raise his arms for an embrace.

When others need to empty their cup, can I be trusted to be present and listen?

May 1

When you make a vow to God, do not delay to fulfill it. For He has no pleasure in fools; what you vow, fulfill. It is better not to vow at all than to vow and not fulfill.

—ECCLESIASTES 5

What would allow me to make only those commitments I can keep?

THE VIRTUE OF TRUSTWORTHINESS

... Trustworthiness is the chief means of attracting confirmation and prosperity. We entreat God to make of it a radiant and mercifully showering rain-cloud that shall bring success and blessings to thy affairs.

—BAHÁ'U'LLÁH

To what extent am I worthy of the trust of others? To what extent am I attracting true success?

May 3

Commitment is inherent in any genuinely loving relationship. Anyone who is truly concerned for the spiritual growth of another knows, consciously or instinctively, that he or she can significantly foster that growth only through a relationship of constancy.

—M. SCOTT PECK

My love is trustworthy. I'm here for the ones I love, and I'm not going anywhere.

May 4

 good name is rather
to be chosen than great riches.

—PROVERBS 22

Never esteem anything
of advantage to you that will make you break your
word or lose your self-respect.

—MARCUS AURELIUS ANTONINUS

*How much value do I place
on keeping my word?*

THE VIRTUE OF TRUSTWORTHINESS

May 5

You are a guardian of the seeds for the world to come. All that has gone before and all that is yet to come is within you. Through you passes humanity's saving fire. You are running in a relay. This is the moment you have been chosen to hold the torch. You cannot refuse to run.

—TOLBERT MCCARROL

How willing am I to carry the trust
only I have been given?

May 6

THE PRACTICE OF TRUSTWORTHINESS

I can be trusted to truly listen.
I only make promises I can keep.
I attract prosperity by being worthy of trust.
My love is committed and constant.
I keep my word.
I treat my gifts as a sacred trust.

I am thankful for the gift of trustworthiness.
It grounds me for true success.

THE VIRTUE OF GRATITUDE

May 7

Lord, I am thankful
for Your love
Your patience
Your tender rebukes
As I slip and slide, meander misty-eyed
in the undergrowth of my illusions
blasting You with infantile rage
when You fail to comply with my Divine expectations.
And You merely side-step gracefully
not looking askance
but grinning a wise and trusting look
at this child-woman
threatened with metamorphosis.
Mother, I am thankful,
for the breast You tender to the child in me,
who will always require succour
And grateful, too, for the times
You send me off, armourless,
to deal with dragons.
Your confidence far exceeds my own.
No box lunch today,
but only the chance for triumph

THE VIRTUE OF GRATITUDE

and the education of deep muscle.
So, I thank You for the caring,
the wounding which heals,
the opportunities to do battle,
and for the fact that always You are there.

—*THANKFUL* BY LINDA KAVELIN POPOV

*What gifts am I most grateful for
in my spiritual growth?*

THE VIRTUE OF GRATITUDE

May 8

hat is to come is better for you than what has gone before: For your Lord will certainly give you, and you will be content . . . Keep recounting the favors of your Lord.

—THE QUR'AN 93

For what has been—thanks!

For what shall be—yes!

—DAG HAMMERSKOLD

Today I count my blessings.
I say yes to the gifts to come.

May 9

... To thank God for His bounties consisteth in possessing a radiant heart, and a soul open to the promptings of the spirit. This is the essence of thanksgiving.

—'ABDU'L-BAHÁ

Every morning, when we wake up, we have twenty-four brand new hours to live. What a precious gift!

—THICH NHAT HAN

Today I am open to the promptings of the spirit.

May 10

No matter what happens always be thankful, for this is God's will for you . . .
                                                    —1 THESSALONIANS 5

I continue to work with the materials I have, the materials I am made of. With feelings, beings, books, events, and battles, I am omnivorous. I would like to swallow the whole earth. I would like to drink the whole sea.

                                                    —PABLO NERUDA

What would free me to work with whatever happens, grateful for my feelings, the events of my life, and especially my spiritual battles?

THE VIRTUE OF GRATITUDE

May 11

There is a quiet humour in Yiddish and a gratitude for every day of life, for every crumb of success, each encounter of love . . . In a figurative way, Yiddish is the wise and humble language of us all, the idiom of a frightened and hopeful humanity.

—ISAAC BASHEVIS SINGER

I am grateful for each and every gift this day holds for me, including humor.

May 12

Normal day, let me be aware of the treasure you are. Let me learn from you, love you, bless you before you depart. Let me not pass you by in quest of some rare and perfect tomorrow. Let me hold you while I may, for it may not always be so. One day I shall dig my nails into the earth, or bury my face in the pillow, or stretch myself taut, or raise my hands to the sky and want, more than all the world, your return.

—MARY JEAN IRON

What is it like for me when I spend a day loving that day, conscious of what a gift it is just to be alive?

THE VIRTUE OF GRATITUDE

May 13

THE PRACTICE OF GRATITUDE

I am grateful for whatever helps my spirit grow.
I count my blessings.
I am open to the promptings of spirit.
I work with what I am given.
I appreciate all that I am given, including
  humor.
I enjoy this particular day.

I am thankful for the gift of gratitude.
It makes my heart sing.

THE VIRTUE OF INTEGRITY

May 14

As a young man, my father went to New York with a dream of becoming an opera singer. He was thrilled when he got a part in the chorus of the Metropolitan Opera. After he and my mother were married, the Depression hit, and he took a job as a secretary in a small commercial real estate firm to make ends meet. Within a few years, he became a partner in the firm. He threw all the passion he had for music into his new career. He initiated bold, innovative and very successful deals, such as the sale of Ebbot's Field, home of the New York Dodgers. He received an award once for "Creative Realtor of the Year." Normally, one associates creativity in that business with something less than virtue, but for my father it wasn't like that. He had a reputation as a man of integrity.

One time a client was visiting, and we all went to the beach on Long Island. As he sat beside my mother on the sand, he talked about the excellent deal my father had negotiated for him. Then he laughed and said, "There's only one thing wrong with your husband. He's too honest." My mother replied, "Would you take your business to anyone else?"

THE VIRTUE OF INTEGRITY

When my father was 82, dying of cancer, we received a deeper awareness of what made him tick. For three days, the family held vigil while he was in a deep coma. Suddenly his voice rang out: "All your life you wander in search of meaning and then, at the end, at the core, there is only the covenant." He had spoken on rare occasions in his life of the covenant between humanity and God. In death, it was his only remaining passion.

What is the covenant I live by?

May 15

Compromise to please others is not as good as integrity that annoys others.
—HUANCHU DAOREN

What you see is what you get.
—ANONYMOUS

What gives me the confidence to be myself and to have integrity no matter what?

THE VIRTUE OF INTEGRITY

May 16

 will sing of loyalty
and justice; to you, O Lord, I will sing.
 I will study the way that is blameless.
 When shall I attain it?
 I will walk with integrity of heart
 within my house;
 I will not set before my eyes
 anything that is base . . .

—PSALM 101

*What do I need to remove from my environ-
ment that interferes with my integrity?*

May 17

Only gradually did I discover what the mandala really is: "Formation, Transformation, Eternal Mind's eternal recreation." And that is the self, the wholeness of the personality, which if all goes well is harmonious, but which cannot tolerate self-deceptions.

—CARL JUNG (QUOTING JOHANN
WOLFGANG VON GOETHE)

What you are speaks so loudly I can't hear what you're saying.

—RALPH WALDO EMERSON

What would allow me to release self-deceptions and move toward wholeness?

May 18

Everyone who hears these words of mine and acts on them will be like a wise man who built his house on rock. The rain fell, the floods came, and the winds blew and beat on that house, but it did not fall, because it had been founded on rock. And everyone who hears these words of mine and does not act on them will be like a foolish man who built his house on sand.

—MATTHEW 7

On what ground am I building my life?

May 19

The key to the mystery of a great artist: that for reasons unknown to him or to anyone else, he will give away his energies and his life just to make sure that one note follows another inevitably. The composer, by doing this, leaves us at the finish with the feeling that something is right in the world, that something checks throughout, something that follows its own laws consistently, something we can trust, that will never let us down.

—LEONARD BERNSTEIN

What calls to me so strongly that I must make sure it is done right?

THE VIRTUE OF INTEGRITY

May 20

THE PRACTICE OF INTEGRITY

I live by my personal covenant.
I am free of the need to please others.
I purify my environment.
I move toward wholeness, shedding my illusions.
I listen to Spirit and stand on solid ground.
I discern the integrity of what I am called to
    create.

I am thankful for integrity.
It is my holy ground.

THE VIRTUE OF JOY

May 21

It was Christmas day. My son sat on the floor, plump little legs splayed, eyes wide and sparkling. He looked up and held his breath as he was handed the gift. He gently touched the bright red ribbon adorning the top, then pulled it off and stuck it on his shirt, looking around proudly. He picked up the box and sucked on one corner. Then with a shout and a wild giggle, began tearing at the shiny paper. He pulled off the top of the box and dumped the tissue paper and what it contained on the floor. After bunching up the paper in his little hands and bending low to hear its crispness, he jumped up, placed the box on his head and paraded around the room. "Honey," his Grandma said, "don't you want your present?" He turned around with a look of surprise, as if to say, "You mean, there's more?"

When do I let myself go with simple joys?

May 22

I like living. I have sometimes been wildly, despairingly, acutely miserable, racked with sorrow, but through it all I still know quite certainly that just to be alive is a grand thing.
—AGATHA CHRISTIE

One ought, every day at least, to hear a little song, read a good poem, see a fine picture, and, if it were possible, to speak a few reasonable words.

—JOHANN WOLFGANG VON GOETHE

*What helps me to be in touch
with the joy of just being alive?*

THE VIRTUE OF JOY

May 23

Joy gives us wings! In times of joy our strength is more vital, our intellect keener, and our understanding less clouded. We seem better able to cope with the world and to find our sphere of influence.

—'ABDU'L-BAHÁ

When has the power of joy
brought me clarity and strength?

THE VIRTUE OF JOY

May 24

ou need not leave your room. Remain sitting at your table and listen. You need not even listen, simply wait. You need not even wait, just learn to become quiet, and still, and solitary. The world will freely offer itself to you to be unmasked. It has no choice; it will roll in ecstasy at your feet.

—FRANZ KAFKA

*How can I design my life to include
the joy of deliberate solitude?*

May 25

e who bends to him-
self a joy
   Doth the winged life destroy;
   But he who kisses the joy as it flies
   Lives in Eternity's sunrise.

—WILLIAM BLAKE

*What would allow me to trust
rather than attempt to control joy?*

May 26

Take delight in the
Lord and he will give you the desires of your heart.

—PSALM 37

Cheer joy is His and
this demands companionship.

—ST. THOMAS AQUINAS

Source of joy, let me keep You company.

May 27

THE PRACTICE OF JOY

I allow myself to enjoy simple pleasures.
I experience the joy of being alive.
Joy brings me clarity.
I find joy in intentional solitude.
I release my need to control joy
Joy is my companion.

I am thankful for the gift of joy.
It is the natural state of my soul.

THE VIRTUE OF COURTESY

May 28

One morning when I asked in meditation, "What virtue do I need with me today?" courtesy came to mind. Later, I went into the office to prepare for some consulting work the next day for the local hospital. Mid-morning, a neighbor telephoned to ask if she could use our photocopier for the Neighborhood Association. "But, I don't want to disturb your important work," she said. I suddenly recalled with a clarity which made me wince several times when she had called or stopped by and I had been brusquely busy, chillingly polite and transparently terse, engaged as I was in "important work." "Please, come by," I said. "It's no trouble."

A couple of hours later, she peeked in the office door and said, "I won't keep you. May I just explain what we need?" "Certainly, Martha," I said, rising from behind my desk and moving forward to greet her. "Would you like some tea?" "Oh, no. I'm in quite a rush myself."

It must have taken all of seven minutes to find out what she needed and to ask about what she was up to that day. "I'm doing my Monday rounds." She explained that each week she would deliver baked goods, warm from her oven, to the long-term care patients and nurses at the hospital.

The next day, I was conducting interviews with the staff of the hospital. When I asked one nurse, "What makes your job easier here?" she smiled and said, "The Cake Lady." Several weeks later, on Martha's eightieth birthday, a surprise party was thrown by a throng of neighbors and friends who came to honor her for her generosity, her service and her being.

When in my life have I interrupted my "important" work to show others the courtesy they deserve?

May 29

Life is not so short but that there is always time enough for courtesy.

—RALPH WALDO EMERSON

In life courtesy and self-possession, and in the arts style, are the sensible impressions of the free mind, for both arise out of a deliberate shaping of all things and from never being swept away, whatever the emotion, into confusion or dullness.

—WILLIAM BUTLER YEATS

What would help me to remember courtesy when my emotions sweep over me?

May 30

O people of God! I admonish you to observe courtesy, for above all else it is the prince of virtues. Well is it with him who is illumined with the light of courtesy and is attired with the vesture of uprightness. Whoso is endued with courtesy hath indeed attained a sublime station. —BAHÁ'U'LLÁH

How much do I value the virtue of courtesy?

THE VIRTUE OF COURTESY

May 31

se a sweet tongue, courtesy, and gentleness, and thou mayest manage to guide an elephant by a hair.

—SA'DI

ee ye not, courtesy
Is the true alchemy,
Turning to gold all it touches and tries?

—GEORGE MEREDITH

*When in my life has a small courtesy
made a big difference?*

THE VIRTUE OF COURTESY

June 1

Let them see no one as their enemy, or as wishing them ill, but think of all humankind as their friends; regarding the alien as an intimate, the stranger as a companion, staying free of prejudice, drawing no lines.

—'ABDU'L-BAHÁ

If a man be gracious and courteous to strangers, it shews he is a citizen of the world, and that his heart is no island cut off from other lands, but a continent that joins them.

—FRANCIS BACON

What would allow me to be gracious and courteous, to strangers as well as to my intimates?

THE VIRTUE OF COURTESY

June 2

f courtesy, it is much
less
    Than courage of the heart or holiness
    Yet in my walks it seems to me
    That the Grace of God is in courtesy.

                  —HILAIRE BELLOC

*Courtesy in my gestures and my speech
is a reflection of Grace.*

THE VIRTUE OF COURTESY

June 3

THE PRACTICE OF COURTESY

Courtesy helps me to honor the dignity of
  others.
Courtesy tames my emotions.
I value the importance of courtesy.
Courtesy empowers me to manage change.
I have an attitude of courtesy toward all people.
Courtesy allows me to be graceful.

I am thankful for the gift of courtesy.
It smoothes the way.

June 4

Dick was one of the most enthusiastic participants in the Virtues Project seminar on parenting. On the third day, he asked to speak to me privately. His face was pale and pinched. "I can't go on with this," he said. I noticed he was shaking. "I can't be . . . a . . . a hypocrite. I just can't get it out of my mind. One night, years ago, when my baby daughter was screaming and wouldn't stop, I took her by the shoulders and I shook her. I shook her so hard. And she was just a baby." Tears coursed down his face.

A few minutes later, we returned to the group. To begin the session, I asked, "How many of you are feeling some grief about abuses or mistakes with your own children?" All hands went up, including mine. Each of us then wrote on a slip of paper, for our eyes only, to be burned that night, the act we most deeply regretted toward our children. We sat together in the circle, silent witnesses to one anothers tears. "When you are ready to let it go, place it in this basket. It will be burned tonight." I stood and prayed aloud "Creator, forgive us, bless these mistakes, make them our teachers. Help us to forgive ourselves, to move forward, ready to change." Then each of us wrote a commitment we would offer in compensation for our mistakes. I wrote "I will trust my children to live by their own process." To my amazement, with no words said about it, a new level of intimacy and trust soon opened up between me and both my sons.

What change will I offer to make amends?

June 5

. . . The angels sing the praises of their Lord, imploring forgiveness for the dwellers of the earth. Is it not that God is forgiving and merciful? . . . He knows the secrets of the hearts. It is He who accepts repentance from His creatures and forgives their trespasses, for He knows what you do.

—THE QUR'AN 42

. . . The most powerful emotions are expressed when the unconditional love of God is accepted by the broken, needy and sinful person.

—DONALD BISSON

I open my heart to Divine forgiveness
and release my unforgiven secrets.

THE VIRTUE OF FORGIVENESS

June 6

If you want to see the brave, look at those who can forgive. If you want to see the heroic, look at those who can love in return for hatred. —THE BHAGAVAD GITA 14

Do not resist an evil-doer. But if anyone strikes you on the right cheek, turn the other also . . . and if anyone forces you to go one mile, go also the second mile.

—MATTHEW 5

What would allow me to detach from conflict, to find the courage to forgive?

THE VIRTUE OF FORGIVENESS

June 7

umility puts an end to
a bad reputation,
self-effort destroys misfortune,
forgiveness destroys anger,
and good conduct wears away undesirable qualities. —THE MAHABHARATA

y friends, if anyone is
detected in a transgression, you who have received
the Spirit should restore such a one in a spirit of
gentleness. —GALATIANS 6

When have I felt anger dissolve
in the gentleness of forgiveness?

June 8

When Peter came to him and asked, 'Lord, how often am I to forgive my brother if he goes on wronging me? As many as seven times?' Jesus replied, 'I do not say seven times but seventy times seven.'

—MATTHEW 18

. . . If a person falls into error for a hundred-thousand times he may yet turn his face to you, hopeful that you will forgive his sins; for he must not become hopeless, neither grieved nor despondent.

—'ABDU'L-BAHÁ

I am willing to keep on forgiving.

June 9

I have learned in recent years that my faults, the defects that keep me from creating the work I want to do, are not flaws or failures. They are wounds. The merest shift in the word shifts attitude. As failures, flaws, defects, I want to crush them underfoot, smash their noses in, impale their heads upon a pike and mount it on the tower wall. But this is my very soul I am impaling there, the essence of my heart. Block, the inability to proceed, signals not a defect but a wound exposed; and curiously in our wounds lie our divinity . . . healing comes from tenderness. Embrace the wounds, wash them, bandage them with loving care . . .   —SOPHY BURNHAM

When have I experienced healing by treating my own wounds tenderly?

June 10

THE PRACTICE OF FORGIVENESS

I make amends for my mistakes.
I accept Divine forgiveness.
I have the humility to forgive others.
I allow forgiveness to dissolve my anger.
I am generous with forgiveness.
I bless my woundedness.

I am thankful for the gift of forgiveness.
It lightens my spirit.

THE VIRTUE OF JUSTICE

June 11

Children love to hear me tell the true story of the curious six-year-old girl who stole a bag of potato chips and ran home in terror to tell her mother. Long before my confession, they whisper conspiratorially, having guessed the thief's identity. I remember my mother's kind, resolute command to return the unopened booty and apologize to the grocer for what I had done. The walk back to the store was interminable. "How did she feel walking back to that store?" I ask. "Scared!" chant the children, their eyes wide in empathy.

I remember how my heart pounded as I re-entered the store. On tip toe, I placed the bag onto the counter and looked up into the grocer's solemn face. "I'm sorry," I cried, a tear sliding down my cheek. "Well now, you're the first one who brought it back." And then he smiled.

"And how did the little girl feel on the way home?" I ask the children. "Happy!" they all shout. "When you do things that you know are wrong, practicing justice helps you to make amends." The children nod wisely.

What mistakes in my life
does justice require me to remedy?

THE VIRTUE OF JUSTICE

June 12

. . . Be custodians of justice [and] witnesses for God even though against your-selves. . . . So follow not the behests of lust lest you swerve from justice.

—THE QUR'AN 4

A man who knows he has committed a mistake and doesn't correct it is committing another mistake.

—CONFUCIUS

What happens when I respect and honor justice by correcting my mistakes? What happens when I don't?

THE VIRTUE OF JUSTICE

June 13

Strive ye then with all your heart to treat compassionately all human-kind—except for those who have some selfish, private motive, or some disease of the soul. Kindness cannot be shown the tyrant, the deceiver, or the thief, because, far from awakening them to the error of their ways, it maketh them to continue in their perversity as before.

—'ABDU'L-BAHÁ

What boundaries does justice require me to set in my life?

THE VIRTUE OF JUSTICE

June 14

omen's question posing when faced with moral conflict indicates a sensitivity to situation and context. . . . They insist on a respectful consideration of the particulars of everyone's needs and frailties, even if that means delaying making decisions or taking action. They do not want to neglect the "practicalities of everyday life" for the sake of abstract justice . . .

In the responsibility orientation to morality, women resolve conflicts not by invoking a logical hierarchy of abstract principles but through trying to understand the conflict in the context of each person's perspective, needs, and goals—and doing the best possible for everyone that is involved. For constructivists, the moral response is the caring response.

—MARY FIELD BELENKEY, ET. AL.

What conflict in my life needs to be resolved in a just and caring way?

June 15

... See that you are merciful . . . deal justly, judge righteously and do good continually; and if ye do all these things shall ye receive your reward . . . ye shall have justice restored unto you again . . . that which ye do send out shall return unto you again, and be restored.

—THE BOOK OF MORMON, ALMA 41

What goes around comes around.

—ANONYMOUS

*How often do I treat others
as I would like to be treated?*

June 16

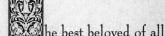he best beloved of all things in My sight is Justice; turn not away therefrom if thou desirest Me, and neglect it not that I may confide in thee. By its aid thou shalt see with thine own eyes and not through the eyes of others, and shalt know of thine own knowledge and not through the knowledge of thy neighbor. Ponder this in thy heart; how it behoveth thee to be. Verily, justice is My gift to thee and the sign of My loving kindness. Set it then before thine eyes.

—BAHÁ'U'LLÁH

What would help me to see with my own eyes, free of the influence of others?

THE VIRTUE OF JUSTICE

June 17

THE PRACTICE OF JUSTICE

I have the courage to face my mistakes.
When I make a mistake, I clean it up.
I set clear boundaries about being treated fairly.
I care about what people really need.
I treat others as I hope to be treated.
I investigate the truth for myself.

I am thankful for the gift of justice.
It keeps me in balance.

THE VIRTUE OF FAITH

June 18

While visiting a U.S. city, I was interviewed on an African American radio show. The producer and I made an immediate personal connection and she invited me to come with her to her church a few days later. I eagerly accepted.

On Sunday morning as we pulled up to park across the street from the church, a chorus of clear voices accompanied by the rhythm of a live band emanated from the small building. It seemed to be rocking on its very foundation. I could feel the pulsating beat of the drums and tambourine as we crossed the threshold.

I was escorted to the front pew and spent the next two hours enveloped in wonderful, lively music and the melifluous voices of various preachers who rose to speak to the congregation. One man asked in a lilting refrain, "Do you say yes to God?" The response from the congregation rose in intensity—"Yes!"

After the service, a lovely, soft-voiced elder offered to drive me back to my hotel. "This is a beautiful car," I said, sitting back on the blue plush seat of her sedan. "Yes," she said, "This is my miracle car." "Oh," I asked, "how so?" "Our minister said to me one day, 'Nelda, it's time for you to get a new car. You don't need to be driving that rickety automobile.' 'Well, I don't have much money.' I said. And the reverend said, 'If it's God's will for you, it will happen.' So then, I just stepped out on the word of God." "What happened?" I asked. She described how she had gone to a car dealer after praying to be led by the will of God. She walked in, told them she needed a new car, the salesman pointed her to this luxurious looking sedan and said, "What can you afford?" It was all over within ten minutes. "That's what happens when you step out on the word of God." she said.

*When have I had the faith
to risk inviting miracles?*

THE VIRTUE OF FAITH

June 19

If ye have faith as a grain of mustard seed, ye shall say unto this mountain, Remove hence to yonder place; and it shall remove; and nothing shall be impossible unto you.

—MATTHEW 17

... Hope cometh of faith, making an anchor for the souls of men, which would make them sure and steadfast ... if there be no faith among the children of men God can do no miracle among them ...

—BOOK OF MORMON, ETHER 12

What blessings have occurred in my life as a result of faith?

THE VIRTUE OF FAITH

June 20

s your faith is, so shall your powers and blessings be.

—'ABDU'L-BAHÁ

t can't be true!" gasped Yellow.

"How can I believe there's a butterfly inside you or me when all I see is a fuzzy worm?" "How does one become a butterfly?" she asked pensively.

"You must want to fly so much that you are willing to give up being a caterpillar."

—TRINA PAULUS

*I have faith that I am capable
of transformation.*

June 21

I do dimly perceive that whilst everything around me is ever changing, ever dying, there is underlying all that change a living power that is changeless, that holds all together, that creates, dissolves, and re-creates. That informing spirit or power is God.

—MAHATMA GHANDI

May we not worry but believe in thee, our great Parent.

—BUNJIRO KAWATE

How can I replace worry with faith in the creative power of change?

THE VIRTUE OF FAITH

June 22

And now here is my secret, a very simple secret; it is only with the heart that one can see rightly, what is essential is invisible to the eye.

—ANTOINE DE SAINT-EXUPÉRY

Faith is the substance of things hoped for, the evidence of things not seen.

—HEBREWS 11

How do things look when I perceive them with my heart?

June 23

Faith is the radical trust that home has always been there and always will be there.

—HENRI J. M. NOUWEN

There is no death. Only a change of worlds.

—CHIEF SEATTLE

Life is a journey which takes me home.

THE VIRTUE OF FAITH

June 24

THE PRACTICE OF FAITH

I welcome miracles.
I believe in great possibilities.
I have faith in my destiny.
I release fear and worry.
My heart knows what is true.
I trust in the journey of life.

I am thankful for the gift of faith.
It is the anchor for my soul.

THE VIRTUE OF IDEALISM

June 25

Martin Luther King, Jr. was a man with a dream. In a speech in Detroit in 1963, he said, "If a man hasn't discovered something that he will die for, he isn't fit to live."

Later that year he led a civil rights march on Washington. When he stood on the platform to speak, arrayed before him was a vast throng of many races. "I have a dream that my four little children will one day live in a nation where they will not be judged by the color of their skin but by the quality of their character."

Years later he spoke to a group of sanitation workers in Tennessee. "Like anybody, I would like to live a long life. Longevity has its place. But I'm not concerned about that now. I just want to do God's will. And He's allowed me to go up to the mountain. And I've looked over, and I've seen the promised land. I may not get there with you, but I want you to know tonight that we as a people will get to the promised land . . . So, I'm happy tonight. I'm not worried about anything. I'm not fearing any man." That was the night before he was assassinated.

What dream do I live for?

—

THE VIRTUE OF IDEALISM

June 26

Where there is no vi-
sion, the people perish. —PROVERBS 29

The difference between
a dream and the vision is the work plan.
—STUART SCHROEDER

Genius is one percent
inspiration and ninety-nine per cent perspiration.
—THOMAS ALVA EDISON

What plan will bring my vision to reality?

June 27

Yes . . . I am very lucky, but I have a little theory about this. I have noticed through experience and through my own observations that Providence, Nature, God, or what I would call the Power of Creation seems to favor human beings who accept and love life unconditionally. And I am certainly one who does, with all my heart. So I have discovered as a result of what I can only call miracles that whenever my inner self desires something subconsciously, life will somehow grant it to me.

—ARTHUR RUBINSTEIN

When have I been able to accept and love life
unconditionally? How much do I believe
in my dreams?

THE VIRTUE OF IDEALISM

June 28

Let your acts be a guide unto all mankind, for the professions of most men, be they high or low, differ from their conduct. It is through your deeds that ye can distinguish yourselves from others. Through them the brightness of your light can be shed upon the whole earth.

—BAHÁ'U'LLÁH

Walk your talk.

—NATIVE AMERICAN PROVERB

To what extent are my actions in alignment with my ideals?

June 29

To be true to the soul is to value the soul, to express it as uniquely as possible. It is loving from inside, rather than accepting a foreign standard that does not take our essence into consideration. To strive for perfection is to kill love because perfection does not recognise humanity. However driven it becomes, the ego cannot achieve its perfectionist ideals because another Reality is within. Nor can it accomplish the task of loving. Only by opening ourselves to the inner Reality do we open ourselves to the possibility of the gift of love. Action and ego choice are involved: we can accept; we can reject; we can withdraw at any point. But we cannot make it happen. Love chooses us. —MARION WOODMAN

What strivings do I need to free myself from in order to be true to my own reality?

June 30

In the city of Brahman
is a secret dwelling,
    the lotus of the heart. Within this dwelling
    is a space, and within that space is the
    fulfillment of our desires. What is within
    that space should be longed for and realised....
    As great as the infinite space beyond is the
    space within the lotus of the heart. Both
    heaven and earth are contained in that inner
space.
    Those who depart from this world . . .
    knowing who they are
    and what they truly desire
    have freedom everywhere,
    both in this world and the next.

—THE CHANDOGYA UPANISHAD

What are the true desires of my heart?

THE VIRTUE OF IDEALISM

July 1

THE PRACTICE OF IDEALISM

I have a dream.
I have a plan.
I have a positive, loving attitude.
I walk my talk.
My ideals are rooted in the real.
I know the true desires of my heart.

I am thankful for idealism.
It is my guiding light.

July 2

One morning, I awoke at dawn and realized it was a holy day, the birthday of the founder of my Faith. I got up, washed my hands and face and went to sit in my prayer chair. I sat in silence for some time watching the sky outside my east-facing window turn rose and crimson. I could feel a prayer forming itself. And then it came. "What can I give you for your birthday, Beloved?" The answer came swiftly. "Your emptiness."

I was puzzled. "Emptiness. What does it mean?" Then, I cupped my hands. I thought of my favorite bowl, one which is so personal no one else in the family uses it. The moment I saw it on the potter's table at an open-air market, I knew it was mine. It is varying shades of blue, lightly glazed, just the right depth and shape for soup or rice. I like the feel of it as I hold it in both hands. I love its perfect, ready emptiness.

As I looked into my cupped hands, it dawned on me—my emptiness is the willingness to receive all that God would give. I felt a Divine smile warming my soul.

How willing am I to receive the gifts of God?

July 3

Go to God as an empty vessel, desiring fulfillment in God's way and measure.

—JOEL S. GOLDSMITH

I want to know God's thoughts . . . the rest are details.

—ALBERT EINSTEIN

Prayer is the contemplation of the facts of life from the highest point of view.

—RALPH WALDO EMERSON

How does my perspective change
when I pray?

July 4

e prayeth best who
loveth best
  All things both great and small;
  For the dear God who loveth us,
  He made and loveth all.

—SAMUEL TAYLOR COLERIDGE

ou pray in your dis-
tress and in your need; would that you might pray
also in the fullness of your joy and in your days of
abundance.   —KAHLIL GIBRAN

*Loving and enjoying life
are good ways for me to pray.*

July 5

Why, O Lord, do you stand far off? Why do you hide yourself in times of trouble?

—PSALM 10

Love Me, that I may love thee. If thou lovest Me not, My love can in no wise reach thee. Know this, O servant.

—BAHÁ'U'LLÁH

When have I been the most open
to the love of my Creator?

July 6

Is prayer your steering wheel or your spare tyre?

—CORRIE TEN BOOM

There are three kinds of souls, three kinds of prayers. One, I am a bow in your hands, Lord, draw me lest I rot. Two, Don't overdraw me Lord or I shall break. Three, Overdraw and who cares if I break. Choose!

—NIKOS KAZENTZAKIS

I trust Divine purpose to guide me.

July 7

Life is fragile—handle
with prayer.
—E. C. MCKENZIE

It is quite possible to
listen to God's voice all through the day without
interrupting your regular activities in any way. The
part of your mind in which truth abides is in constant communication with God, whether you are
aware of it or not. —A COURSE IN MIRACLES 2

*What simple practices would allow me to
listen to Spirit throughout the day?*

THE VIRTUE OF PRAYERFULNESS

July 8

THE PRACTICE OF PRAYERFULNESS

I create sacred space in my life to receive
    abundance.
I uplift my perspective through prayer.
I am thankful for the gifts in my life.
Prayer heals my loneliness.
I trust my life to Divine purpose.
I listen to Spirit throughout the day.

I am thankful for the gift of prayerfulness.
It engages my soul.

THE VIRTUE OF GENTLENESS

July 9

On Saturday morning, Joey knelt on the couch, nose pressed against the window.

"Mom, when Grampa comin?"

"Soon, Sweetheart."

Finally, the battered brown Dodge rolled into the driveway.

"Mom, Grampa here!" Joey raced outside and flung himself into the old man's arms.

"Are we gonna have a aventure today?"

"Sure, Joey. How about a safari?"

They walked, hand in hand, to the park, continually on the look-out for creatures and beasts.

Joey stalked squirrels, climbed the jungle gym, played with some "big boys" and swung "as high as a mountain. Right, Grampa?"

After they watched a colony of ants hard at work, Grandfather said quietly, "Time to go, Joe."

Joey started to complain then looked up at Grandfather's face and thought better of it.

Hand in hand, they started homeward across the grassy expanse. Suddenly Joey spotted something moving in the grass.

THE VIRTUE OF GENTLENESS

"Look, Grampa!" They knelt down and saw a baby bird, wobbling in the grass. Joey reached out for it.

"No!" said Grandfather, firmly.

"Why, Grampa? I jus' wanna touch it."

"It's sick, Joey, and it could be easily hurt. We need to be kind to it."

A tear slid down the boy's face. "I won't hurt it"

"Can you be very, very gentle?"

Joey nodded vigorously. "I be gentle." He reached out one pudgy finger and slowly, softly stroked the little feathered back. His eyes shone.

Once they reached the house, Joey barreled through the door and threw his arms around his mother's knees.

"How was your adventure, Sweetheart?"

"Mom, I was gentle!"

*When have I given the gift of gentleness
to one who was wounded?*

July 10

soft answer turns
away wrath,
   but a harsh word stirs up anger.

—PROVERBS 15

o not speak harshly to
anybody; those who are spoken to will answer thee
in the same way. Angry speech breeds trouble, thou
wilt receive blows for blows.

—THE DHAMMAPADA

*What difference does it make when I respond
with gentleness instead of anger?*

July 11

Be swift to hear, slow to speak, slow to wrath.
—JAMES 1:19

May you always listen, always hear, always speak with the power of the spirit.
—'ABDU'L-BAHÁ

I have the power to listen quietly and respond gently in every situation.

THE VIRTUE OF GENTLENESS

July 12

The great of earth
How softly do they live;
The lesser ones are praised,
Revered;
Still lesser, feared;
But these,
One hardly knows that they are there,
So gently do they go about their tasks,
So quietly achieve;
When they have passed,
Their life's work done,
The people look and say:
It happened of itself . . .

—RUTH TENNEY (BASED ON A POEM BY LAO TZE)

How great can my achievements be when my actions flow from gentleness?

THE VIRTUE OF GENTLENESS

July 13

From below the silence a strong, sweet feeling began to rise. I was meeting the center of the earth and she was love, a love which supported and embraced everything without exception. A love which drew back from nothing, no matter how horrible. I wept with gratitude as that love enfolded me. I understood with my whole body how ridiculous it was for me to strain to hold myself up. All my life I had been completely supported by this love at the center of the earth, but I hadn't noticed because I was always trying to rise above life. I could have surrendered to it. I could have nestled into this mother's arms and lived there safely. I felt compassion and pity for my lifetime of needless, exhausting striving.

—SHERRY RUTH ANDERSON & PATRICIA HOPKINS

I release needless strain. I surrender to the gentle, tender love which has always been there for me.

July 14

here is something in angling . . . that tends to produce a gentleness of spirit, and a pure serenity of mind.

—WASHINGTON IRVING

loafe and invite my soul,
   I lean and loafe at my ease observing a spear of summer grass.

—WALT WHITMAN

What simple activities restore the gentleness in my spirit?

THE VIRTUE OF GENTLENESS

July 15

THE PRACTICE OF GENTLENESS

I am gentle with those who are wounded.
I speak with gentleness.
I listen with gentleness.
My actions flow from gentleness.
I nurture myself with gentleness.
Gentle activities restore my spirit.

I am thankful for gentleness.
It brings peace to my soul.

July 16

Maggie was assigned to the inner city classroom in the middle of the year. All the principal had told her was that the former teacher had left suddenly, and that this was a class of "special" students. She walked in on bedlam, spitballs flying through the air, feet on desks, the noise deafening. She walked to the front of the classroom and opened the attendance book. She looked down the list of names and saw beside them numbers from 140 to 160. "Oh," she thought to herself. "No wonder they are so high-spirited. These children have exceptional I.Q.s." She smiled and brought them to order.

At first, the students failed to turn in work. Assignments that were handed in were done hastily and sloppily. She began to speak to them about their innate excellence, their giftedness, that she expected nothing short of the best work from them. She kept reminding them of their responsibility to use all the extra intelligence God had given them. Things began to change. The children sat up tall, they worked diligently. Their work was creative, precise, original. One day, the principal was walking by and happened to look into the classroom. He observed students in rapt attention, composing essays.

THE VIRTUE OF EXCELLENCE

Later, he called Maggie into his office. "What have you done to these kids?" he asked. "Their work has surpassed all the regular grades." "Well, what do you expect? They're gifted, aren't they?" "Gifted?! They're the special-needs students—behavioral disordered and retarded." "Then why are their IQs so high on the attendance sheet?" "Those aren't their IQs. Those are their locker numbers!"

"Whatever," said Maggie.

How often do I expect the best from others and myself?

July 17

e created man of finest possibilities.

—THE QUR'AN 95

 teacher who can arouse a feeling for one single good action, for one single good poem, accomplishes more than he who fills our memory with rows on rows of natural objects, classified with name and form.

—JOHANN WOLFGANG VON GOETHE

What excellent possibilities
am I called to fulfill?

July 18

ost thou reckon thy-
self only a puny form
    When within thee the universe is folded?

—IMAM ALI

What you are is much
greater than anything or anyone else you have ever
yearned for. God is manifest in you in a way that
He is not manifest in any other human being. Your
face is unlike anyone else's, your soul is unlike
anyone else's, you are sufficient unto yourself; for
within your soul lies the greatest treasure of all—
God.   —PARAMAHANSA YOGANANDA

How content am I to be who I am?

July 19

A master in the art of living draws no sharp distinction between her work and her play, her labour and her leisure, her mind and her body, her education and her recreation. She hardly knows which is which. She simply pursues her vision of excellence through whatever she is doing and leaves others to determine whether she is working or playing. To herself she always seems to be doing both. —ANONYMOUS

I find the joy in all that I do,
and it leads me to excellence.

July 20

Each of you should examine your own conduct, and then he can measure his achievement by comparing himself to himself and not with anyone else; for everyone has his own burden to bear.   —GALATIANS 6

What achievements have meant the most to me?

July 21

. . . In every art and skill, God loveth the highest perfection.

—BAHÁ'U'LLÁH

We shall give more excellence to him who acquires excellence.

—THE QUR'AN 42

What happens when I give my best to my work and my relationships?

THE VIRTUE OF EXCELLENCE

July 22

THE PRACTICE OF EXCELLENCE

I expect excellence from others and myself.
I fulfill my true possibilities.
I value my unique gifts.
I enjoy what I am doing and excellence follows.
I set my own standards.
I give my best to all that I do.

I am thankful for the gift of excellence.
It adds value to my life.

THE VIRTUE OF WISDOM

July 23

I was floored when I was asked to make a spiritual care visit to a man in a deep coma. He had been brought in by ambulance the night before after a third attempted suicide. I had never met him before and was at a loss as to how to help. As I approached the busy intensive care ward, I prayed "I have no idea what to do for this man. Please give me the wisdom to be of some use to him."

I found Joseph in a bed placed in the center of a busy ward, nurses and doctors bustling around. He was hooked up to life support machines but completely unconscious. Although his chest moved up and down in perfect rhythm, he seemed lifeless. I spoke to him and touched his hand with no response. Suddenly, to my great embarrassment, I felt moved to sing! I leaned close to his ear and hummed an unfamiliar tune. A tear slid out of the corner of his closed eye. I felt what I can only describe as an enormous bolt of energy connecting the two of us.

Days later, I went to see him in the psychiatric ward where he had been placed after refusing to agree not to make another suicide attempt. He told me that he was dying of ALS (Lou Gehrig's Disease) and had no desire to "die a slow death." The most devastating part for him was losing the use of his hands. I listened a long time and then asked him: "Do you remember hearing my voice when you were in coma?" "No," he said, "it's all a blank." "Well, it was the strangest thing. I sang this song to you." I hummed the melody. He grinned deeply at me, his first and only smile. "Well, that was my favorite song as a child. Music is the only way you could have reached me. You see, I'm a musician."

When have I had the courage to act on the wisdom of my intuition?

THE VIRTUE OF WISDOM

July 24

I think the most wonderful things in life are beyond reason, that is why I think "why" is often such an irrelevant question, it is very limited. The real things of life have nothing to do with "why." They are just "so," they are just "thus." Life is a "thus," and until you realize this "thusness" of life you are stuck.

—LAURENS VAN DER POST

There sometimes seems to be an inverse relationship between information and wisdom. —THOMAS MOORE

When have I gotten beyond reason to experience the essence of life?

July 25

o not be afraid to em-
brace the arms
of loneliness.
Do not be concerned with the thorns
of solitude.
Why worry that you will miss something?
Learn to be at home with yourself
without a hand to hold.
Learn to endure isolation
with only the stars for friends . . .
Solitude
brings the clarity of still waters.
Wisdom
completes the circle of your dreams.

—NANCY WOOD

*How do I need to design my time
to include stillness and solitude?*

July 26

I, Wisdom, am mistress of discretion, the inventor of lucidity of thought.

Good advice and sound judgement belong to me, perception to me, strength to me . . .

The fruit I give is better than gold, even the finest, the return I make is better than pure silver.

I walk in the way of virtue,
in the paths of justice,
enriching those who love me,
filling their treasuries.

—PROVERBS 8

*When have I called on wisdom
to clear up my thinking?*

July 27

As by knowing one lump of clay, dear one,
We come to know all things made out of clay—
That they differ only in name and form,
While the stuff of which all are made is clay; . . .
So through spiritual wisdom, dear one,
We come to know that all of life is one.

—THE CHANDOGYA UPANISHAD

Through the eyes of wisdom,
I see all life as one.

July 28

. . . If you accept my words
And treasure my commandments;
If you make your ears attentive to wisdom
And your minds open to discernment;
If you call to understanding
And cry aloud to discernment,
If you seek it as you do silver
And search for it as for treasures,
Then you will understand the fear of the Lord
and attain knowledge of God.

—PROVERBS 2

What decisions in my life
call for wise discernment?

THE VIRTUE OF WISDOM

July 29

THE PRACTICE OF WISDOM

I am willing to act on the wisdom of my
intuition.
I allow the wisdom of my soul to take me beyond
reason.
I discover my wisdom in stillness and solitude.
Wisdom gives me lucidity of thought.
Through wisdom I see the oneness of life.
I make decisions by being attentive to wisdom
and discernment.

I am thankful for the gift of wisdom.
It leads me to clarity.

THE VIRTUE OF COURAGE

July 30

"So you think I'm courageous?" she asked.

"Yes, I do."

"Perhaps I am. But that's because I've had some in-spiring teachers. I'll tell you about one of them. Many years ago, when I worked as a volunteer at Stanford Hospital, I got to know a little girl named Liza who was suffering from a rare and serious disease. Her only chance of recovery appeared to be a blood transfusion from her five-year-old brother who had miraculously survived the same disease and had developed the antibodies needed to combat the illness. The doctor explained the situation to her little brother, and asked the boy if he would be willing to give his blood to his sister. I saw him hesitate for only a moment before taking a deep breath and say-ing, 'Yes, I'll do it if it will save Liza.'

"As the transfusion progressed, he lay in a bed next to his sister and smiled, as we all did, seeing the color returning to her cheeks. Then his face grew pale and his smile faded. He looked up at the doctor and asked with a trembling voice, 'Will I start to die right away?'

"Being young, the boy had misunderstood the doc-tor; he thought he was going to have to give her all his blood. "Yes, I've learned courage," she added, "because I've had inspiring teachers."

—DAN MILLMAN

*Who have been my most inspiring
teachers of courage?*

THE VIRTUE OF COURAGE

July 31

hen I called, You an-
swered me,
 You inspired me with courage.

—PSALM 138

trive as much as ye
can to turn wholly toward the Kingdom, that ye
may acquire innate courage and ideal power.

—'ABDU'L-BAHÁ

*When have I needed the most courage and
what gave me the strength to act on it?*

THE VIRTUE OF COURAGE

August 1

We cannot escape fear.
We can only transform it into a companion that
accompanies us on all our exciting adventures . . .
Take a risk a day—one small or bold stroke that
will make you feel great once you have done it.

—SUSAN JEFFERS

*What risk can I take now
to transform fear into courage?*

August 2

It takes so much to be a full human being that there are very few who have the enlightenment or courage to pay full price. One has to abandon altogether the search for security and reach out to the risk of living with both arms. One has to embrace the world like a lover. One has to accept pain as a condition of existence. One has to court doubt and darkness as the cost of knowing. One needs a will stubborn in conflict but apt always to total acceptance of every consequence of living and dying.

—MORRIS L. WEST

Heart, be brave. If you cannot be brave, just go. Love's glory is not a small thing.

—JALAL'U'DIN RUMI

What do I love so much
that I am willing to just go for it?

THE VIRTUE OF COURAGE

August 3

Life shrinks or expands in proportion to one's courage.

—ANAÏS NIN

There is the risk you cannot afford to take [and] there is the risk you cannot afford not to take.

—PETER DRUCKER

What risks am I called to take in my life every day?

THE VIRTUE OF COURAGE

August 4

But indeed if any show patience and forgive, that would truly be an exercise of courageous will and resolution in the conduct of affairs. —THE QUR'AN 42

With courage, you will dare to take risks, have the strength to be compassionate and the wisdom to be humble. Courage is the foundation of integrity.

—KESHAVAN NAIR

Who and what do I have the courage
to forgive?

August 5

THE PRACTICE OF COURAGE

I have the courage to sacrifice for what I love.
I find courage in prayer.
Courage transforms my fears.
I have the courage to embrace life fully.
I have the courage to take risks.
I have the courage to be compassionate.

I am thankful for the gift of courage.
It is my launching pad.

THE VIRTUE OF PERSEVERANCE

August 6

Well, son, I'll tell you:
Life for me ain't been no crystal stair.
It's had tacks in it.
And splinters,
And boards torn up,
And places with no carpet on the floor—
Bare.
But all the time
I'se been a-climbin' on,
And reachin' landins
And turnin' corners,
And sometimes goin' in the dark
Where there ain't been no light.
So, boy, don't you turn back,
Don't you set down on the steps
'Cause you finds it's kinder hard.
Don't you fall now—
For I'se still goin' honey,
I'se still climbin'
And life for me ain't been no crystal stair.

—*MOTHER TO SON* BY LANGSTON HUGHES

*What tests in my life
have taught me perseverance?*

August 7

The sense of obligation to continue is present in all of us. A duty to strive is the duty of us all. I felt a call to that duty.

—ABRAHAM LINCOLN

Keep on keepin' on.

—AFRICAN-AMERICAN SAYING

*What in my life calls for the perseverance
to continue?*

THE VIRTUE OF PERSEVERANCE

August 8

I have heard that an eagle misses seventy per cent of its strikes. Why should I expect to do better? And when he misses, does he scold himself, I wonder, for failing at the task?

... the only element I find common to all successful writers is persistence—an overwhelming determination to succeed. . . . They will not be thrust aside!   —SOPHY BURNHAM

*In what arena have I had the perseverance
to succeed?*

August 9

O you who believe, seek courage in fortitude and prayer, for God is with those who are patient and persevere.

—THE QUR'AN 2

W here is thy faith? Stand firmly and with perseverance; take courage and be patient; comfort will come to thee in due time.

—THOMAS À KEMPIS

I trust that if I have faith and perseverance, any problem can be solved.

August 10

Nothing in the world can take the place of Persistence. Talent will not; nothing is more common than unsuccessful men with talent. Genius will not; unrewarded genius is almost a proverb. Education alone will not; the world is full of educated derelicts. Persistence and determination alone are omnipotent.

—ANONYMOUS

What talents require me to persevere?

THE VIRTUE OF PERSEVERANCE

August 11

Spirit who comes out
of the East,
come to me with the power of the rising sun.
Let there be light in my word.
Let there be light on the path that I walk.
Let me remember always that you give the gift
of a new day.
Never let me be burdened with sorrow by not
starting over.

—EXCERPT FROM "LET ME WALK IN BEAUTY,"
NATIVE AMERICAN TRADITION

What is the source of my perseverance?

THE VIRTUE OF PERSEVERANCE

August 12

THE PRACTICE OF PERSEVERANCE

I have the perseverance to overcome obstacles.
I have the will to carry on.
I am determined to succeed.
I have faith that a way will be found.
Perseverance brings my gifts to fruition.
I have the perseverance to start over.

I am thankful for perseverance.
It keeps me going.

THE VIRTUE OF BEAUTY

August 13

The first time I met Mary, a lovely woman of sixty-three who was dying of emphysema, she quoted a verse from Proverbs to me. "'In all her ways are pleasantness and all her paths are peace.' I am simply haunted by the beauty of those words," she said. As her physical condition deteriorated, she could hardly get enough breath to speak, but one day she whispered. "People feel sorry for old people. But they don't understand. They don't know . . . there are things . . . wonderful things." "What things, Mary?" Her eyes were luminous. "Words," she said, "the beauty of words." One day, it occurred to me to ask her if she had ever done any writing. She blushed shyly. I asked to see something she had written. The old brown envelope was full of poems and short stories in faded type. I especially remember one of a young soldier who came for tea. I could see in my imagination the translucency of the cup he held and the slight tremor of his hand.

I had the privilege of being with Mary the day she died. The nurses said she wasn't recognizing anyone and that she was in a strange state of agitation. Her relatives were taking a break and I found her alone when I walked into the room. Her eyes fastened on mine and I said softly. "Words, Mary, the beauty of words. 'In all her ways are pleasantness and all her paths are peace.'" She gave me a radiant smile and, soon after, she went.

What most evokes my love for beauty?

August 14

The perception of beauty is a moral test.

—HENRY DAVID THOREAU

What is beautiful is moral, that is all there is to it.

—GUSTAVE FLAUBERT

*How does my sense of beauty
illumine my sense of values?*

August 15

f there is light in the soul,

    There will be beauty in the person.
    If there is beauty in the person,
    There will be harmony in the house.
    If there is harmony in the house,
    There will be order in the nation.
    If there is order in the nation,
    There will be peace in the world.

—CHINESE PROVERB

*Which aspects of my life best reflect
beauty and order?*

THE VIRTUE OF BEAUTY

August 16

 thing of beauty is a
joy forever:
   Its loveliness increases; it will never
   Pass into nothingness: but will still keep
   A bower of quiet for us, and a sleep
   Full of sweet dreams, and health, and quiet
   breathing.   —JOHN KEATS

*What would it take for me to create an
environment of quiet beauty in my home?*

THE VIRTUE OF BEAUTY

August 17

The human soul needs actual beauty more than bread.

—D. H. LAWRENCE

The most beautiful thing we can experience is the mysterious. It is the source of all true art and science.

—ALBERT EINSTEIN

*How often do I feed my soul
with an experience of beauty?*

August 18

ne thing I ask of the
Lord,
    that I will seek after:
    to live in the house of the Lord
    all the days of my life,
    to behold the beauty of the Lord . . .

—PSALM 27

he lover's teacher is
the loved one's beauty.   —THE MATHNAVI

I am inspired by the beauty
of Divine mystery.

THE VIRTUE OF BEAUTY

August 19

THE PRACTICE OF BEAUTY

I reflect on what is beautiful to me.
Beauty illumines my true values.
Beauty within me brings peace to the world.
I will create an environment of beauty.
I am open to the beauty of mystery.
Divine beauty is my inspiration.

I am thankful for the gift of beauty.
It nourishes my soul.

THE VIRTUE OF SACRIFICE

August 20

When he was four years old, my son Christopher was a dedicated miser. He collected money. He hunted for it under couch cushions, on the street, in the park. He unabashedly solicited hand-outs from visiting uncles, showed up at "allowance time" like clock-work, and then, repeatedly and carefully counted the small weekly sum. He preferred to receive it in the smallest denominations— nickels instead of dimes, pennies instead of nickels—because it was "more." He did extra chores to add to his booty. He kept it stashed in a blue velvet bag, which had originally contained a gift bottle of cologne. He spent hours counting out his money, announcing each increase in his fortune with great pride. It actually had me a little worried. He refused to spend it and at times went without ice cream or some other treat he really wanted.

One evening, a television documentary came on about a drought in Africa. I got up to change the channel, wondering if this would be appropriate for Christopher to see. He said, "Leave it, Mommy. I want to see." I thought perhaps it would be valuable for him to learn of the troubles of people across the world. He was mesmerized by the scenes of emaciated children crying in hunger. At the end of the show, there was a pledge campaign. Christopher went running from the room and returned, carrying his blue bag. He placed it on my lap and said, "Mommy, can I send this to those children?" "Yes, Chris, you can." "Then, send it, Mommy," he said. "All of it."

When have I sacrificed something I really cared about for something I cared about more?

August 21

We need people who will dare to risk anything and everything to see things different.
—SHUSHOBHA BARVE

Art is unthinkable without risk and spiritual self-sacrifice.
—BORIS PASTERNAK

What do I care about so much that I dare to risk anything for it?

August 22

The true seeker hunteth naught but the object of his quest, and the lover hath no desire save union with his beloved. Nor shall the seeker reach his goal unless he sacrifice all things. That is, whatever he hath seen, and heard, and understood, all must he set at naught, that he may enter the realm of the spirit, which is the City of God. Labor is needed, if we are to seek Him; ardor is needed, if we are to drink of the honey of reunion with Him; and if we taste of this cup, we shall cast away the world.

—BAHÁ'U'LLÁH

What am I truly seeking in my life?

THE VIRTUE OF SACRIFICE

August 23

If any want to become my followers, let them deny themselves and take up their cross daily and follow me. For those who want to save their life will lose it, and those who lose their life for my sake will save it. What does it profit them if they gain the whole world, but lose or forfeit themselves.

—LUKE 9

. . . If your goal is to avoid pain and escape suffering, I would not advise you to seek higher levels of consciousness or spiritual evolution.

—M. SCOTT PECK

For what purpose have I been willing to endure pain?

August 24

f you are following your truest desire, you will look for every occasion possible to work away at your dream. I work extremely long hours, because I love to and choose to. Follow your desire, it is heavenly fire.

—SUZANNE NADON

What sacrifices am I called to make to follow my truest desire?

August 25

othing is small if God
accepts it.
—ST. TERESA OF AVILA

an discovers his own
wealth
When God comes to ask gifts from him.
—RABINDRANATH TAGORE

What activities can be made holy today
by dedicating them to God?

THE VIRTUE OF SACRIFICE

August 26

THE PRACTICE OF SACRIFICE

Generosity leads me to sacrifice.
I take risks for what I care about.
I am a true seeker of truth.
I embrace the pain of transformation.
I give what my dreams require.
I dedicate my actions to the Creator.

I am thankful for the gift of sacrifice.
It makes sacred what I have to give.

THE VIRTUE OF TOLERANCE

August 27

When Jonas was seven years old, a serious illness swept through his northern Alberta village, killing both his parents and most of his relatives. He was placed in a foster home with a family many miles away. After a few weeks, his foster mother called Alice, the social worker who had placed the boy. "This boy is a thief. . . He just helps himself to whatever he wants. He goes into my son's room, takes his clothes, steals food at night, just takes without asking. I don't know if we can keep him here." Alice drove out to investigate. When Jonas came home from school, she took him for a ride and asked him how it was going. "They don't like me," said the boy and he began to cry. He was very confused by the family's anger at him. They drove back to the house and she sent him out to play.

The two women sat down over a cup of tea. Alice explained that in the First Nation village where Jonas was raised, the children were raised by everyone. "If you sleep overnight at your cousins' house, you just wear their clothes to school the next day. They do the same when they come to your house. The meals are not always at a certain time, so the children are encouraged to take food when they are hungry. Jonas is a good boy. He is just practicing the sharing tradition of his people. And he can learn your ways of sharing if you explain them." Tears filled the foster mother's eyes. "I just didn't know." As the women embraced, Alice knew that Jonas would be all right here after all.

When have I been willing to develop tolerance by appreciating differences?

August 28

et yourselves be divested of prejudice.

If you are good scholars, you learn to treat your neighbours as they should be treated, and to have the same affections for a person from Ireland or England as you do for one from your own native land.   —BRIGHAM YOUNG

What preconceptions do I need to let go of to divest myself from prejudice?

August 29

Judge not, that ye be not judged.

—MATTHEW 7

Nothing keeps people together like the exalted conviction that they alone are to be spared that eternal anguish of hell fire to which everyone else will be condemned at a rapidly approaching Day of Judgement.

—PHILIP TOYNBEE

*When has tolerance set me free
from my judgements?*

August 30

Be tolerant of one another and forgiving, if any of you has cause for complaint: you must forgive as the Lord forgave you.
—COLOSSIANS 3

Time will bring healing.
—EURIPIDES

What can tolerance help me to forgive?

THE VIRTUE OF TOLERANCE

August 31

...The heaven of true understanding shineth resplendent with the light of two luminaries: tolerance and righteousness.

—BAHÁ'U'LLÁH

In my relationships, where is the balance between being tolerant and standing up for what is right and just?

THE VIRTUE OF TOLERANCE

September 1

The anguish washes over
    like floods over dry land,
    soaking each crevice
    soaking into my soul.
    But my private joy
    my knowing of unique ecstasy
    is enriched
    by the stark and singular contrast
    of pure joy, and pain
    With time, pain relinquishes to sadness.
    Joy becomes fond memory.
    Anguish,
    having watered the soul
    brings new sustenance
    to those seeds already sown
    of spirit and of strength.

—SUSAN D. RUSSELL

When have the sorrows of my life brought
new sustenance to my soul?

THE VIRTUE OF TOLERANCE

THE PRACTICE OF TOLERANCE

I appreciate differences.

I divest myself of prejudice.

I am free of judgements.

I am able to forgive.

I balance tolerance and righteousness in my
   relationships.

I embrace the joy and the pain of my life.

*I am thankful for the gift of tolerance.
It broadens my horizons.*

THE VIRTUE OF ENTHUSIASM

At the closing circle of the retreat, each of the ten women shared a symbol of herself. Annie was the last to speak. "I guess it's my turn," she said. Her plain, ruddy face was slightly swollen from unaccustomed tears, her eyes bright. Although she was the oldest woman there, she was new to this sort of sharing. It was the first time she had ever told anyone about her years in an abusive marriage and the courage it took for her to take her six children and leave. For her, taking this weekend for herself was an almost unimaginable indulgence. She savored everything—the women's stories, the food, the music, the laughter, and most of all, her own free-flowing tears.

She placed a small block of wood in the center of the circle. Her face was flushed, radiant. "I couldn't think of anything, but then I noticed this lying in the yard. It's just like me. It's simple, a bit crude, it's not perfect, and it's not finished. But, oh, the possibilities!"

What possibilities fill me with enthusiasm?

THE VIRTUE OF ENTHUSIASM

September 4

When you discard arrogance, complexity, and a few other things that get in the way, sooner or later you will discover that simple, childlike and mysterious secret known to those of the Uncarved Block: Life is Fun ... From the state of the Uncarved Block comes the ability to enjoy the simple and the quiet, the natural and the plain. Along with that comes the ability to do things spontaneously and have them work, odd as that may appear to others at times.

—BENJAMIN HOFF

When in my life do I allow myself to be
present to the natural and the plain,
to simply have fun?

THE VIRTUE OF ENTHUSIASM

September 5

Develop interest in life as you see it; in people, things, literature, music— the world is so rich, simply throbbing with rich treasures, beautiful souls and interesting people. Forget yourself. —HENRY MILLER

When has enthusiasm for the richness of life led me beyond my narrow concerns?

THE VIRTUE OF ENTHUSIASM

September 6

ook within.
Be still.
Free from fear and attachment,
Know the sweet joy of the way.

—THE DHAMMAPADA 15

n·thu·si·asm, n. 1.a.
Rapturous interest or excitement. b. Ardent fond-
ness. 2. Something that inspires a lively interest.
[Gk *enthousiazein*, to be inspired by God.]

—THE AMERICAN HERITAGE DICTIONARY

How much of my enthusiasm
comes from being inspired within?

THE VIRTUE OF ENTHUSIASM

September 7

And whatsoever ye do, do it heartily . . . —COLOSSIANS 3

Work of any kind, if done in the right spirit, gives you victory over yourself . . . The attitude with which you work is what counts. —PARAMAHANSA YOGANANDA

What would allow me to love my work wholeheartedly?

THE VIRTUE OF ENTHUSIASM

September 8

To be successful, the first thing to do is fall in love with your work.

—SISTER MARY LAURETTA

It don't mean a thing if it ain't got that swing.

—DUKE ELLINGTON & IRVING MILLS

What kind of work makes my heart sing?

THE VIRTUE OF ENTHUSIASM

September 9

THE PRACTICE OF ENTHUSIASM

I am excited by possibilities.
I enjoy simple, spontaneous fun.
I treasure my life.
My enthusiasm comes from within.
I love what I do.
I do what I love.

I am thankful for enthusiasm.
It makes life simply wonderful.

THE VIRTUE OF COMMITMENT

September 10

"**Y**ou like working with the dying?" people used to ask me with surprise when I served as Spiritual Care Coordinator at a Hospice. The truth is I loved it! I felt like a privileged midwife to people in the most important transition of their lives. To walk intimately and contemplatively with them in their most fragile and powerful hours filled me with wonder. While working at Hospice half-time, I had also coauthored *The Virtues Guide*. Requests for presentations began flooding in from schools, churches, government agencies. It was joyful work, assisting people to awaken to their spirituality. I started traveling and juggling my hours at Hospice more and more. How was I to keep from burning out, being torn by these two commitments I loved?

I gave myself a rare gift—a whole day for prayer and discernment. I sat outside in the yard on the warm sunlit earth and closed my eyes. Once my spirit quieted down into silence, I heard the familiar voice that often comes in prayer. "You will be offered a job. You are not to take it. I have other things for you to do." This sounded strange. Another job? My problem was the two I already had. "Is that imagination or guidance?" I wondered. The next day, out of the blue, the President of the Hospice Board asked me to lunch. He offered me an executive position. I blushed and blurted out, "No!" More gently, I explained, "I have other things to do" and told him about The Virtues Project. "Oh, that'll never fly," he said. The next week, I resigned from Hospice to tend to The Virtues Project full time. Since then, it has flown me around the world.

When have I felt called to give up the important for the most important commitment?

THE VIRTUE OF COMMITMENT

September 11

. . . If ye remain firm and act aright . . . your Lord would help you with five thousand angels . . . —THE QUR'AN 3

Until one is committed there is hesitancy, the chance to draw back, always ineffectiveness. Concerning all acts of initiative and creation there is one elementary truth, the ignorance of which kills countless ideas and splendid plans; that the moment one definitely commits oneself, then Providence moves too. All sorts of things occur to one that would never otherwise have occurred . . . whatever you can do, or dream you can . . . begin it. Boldness has genius, power, and magic in it. —JOHANN WOLFGANG VON GOETHE

When have I been aware of Providence moving in my life?

September 12

But for the tribulations which are sustained in Thy path, how could Thy true lovers be recognized . . .

—BAHÁ'U'LLÁH

When we are on the verge of making a deep promise, it is not uncommon for great resistances and fears to arise. Whatever threatens our reality or present way of life, whatever we know will profoundly change us, often seems more terrifying than inviting. But if we are able to make the commitment, we sometimes experience an unexpected joy.

—SHERRY RUTH ANDERSON & PATRICIA HOPKINS

What in me resists transformation and commitment?

September 13

By their fruits ye shall know them.

—MATTHEW 7

Commitment isn't something that just happens by chance. Commitment is a capacity, and it grows as a muscle grows, by being exercised.

—CHARLOTTE JOLLO BECK

What have been the fruits of my willingness to commit?

THE VIRTUE OF COMMITMENT

September 14

 ow a thought, and you
reap an act;
   Sow an act, and you reap a habit;
   Sow a habit, and you reap a character;
   Sow a character, and you reap a destiny.

—ANONYMOUS

eep your eyes on the
prize.   —ALCOHOLICS ANONYMOUS SLOGAN

What thought is the focus
of my commitment?

September 15

Don't think you understand, there is no understanding, there is jumping into the fire, there is stripping for the Beloved, there is a cry of joy, a wild act of lovemaking with the Divine Spirit, but don't call that understanding, don't try to wrap it around a formula; that won't help you, that will prevent you from being helped.

—ANDREW HARVEY

When I hear the call of the Beloved,
I am ready to move.

THE VIRTUE OF COMMITMENT

THE PRACTICE OF COMMITMENT

I am ready to commit to my highest calling.
I am open to Divine assistance.
I have the courage to face my resistance.
I am willing to stretch and grow.
I am guided by a clear vision.
I surrender to the passion of my soul.

I am thankful for commitment.
It focuses my life.

THE VIRTUE OF SERVICE

September 17

"What are you doing this weekend?" I asked Rita during our walk. "You won't believe it," she laughed "milking cows!" "You're doing what?" "Well, this young couple need a break. They haven't had a holiday for years. So, I'm just going to clean out their stalls and milk their cows, keep an eye on things." I smiled at her. "You're always up to something, aren't you? Always taking care of people." "Oh, well . . . " She brushed off the threat of praise.

As we walked along the dappled forest path in silence, my mind drifted back to the time when Rita had taken care of me. Hardly anyone knew of my private grieving. Yet she sensed it and asked me to dinner. "Got to fatten you up," she said, "you're looking a bit thin." After a delicious vegetable stew, we settled onto the couch over steaming cups of tea and she asked, "So, what is it, Sweetie?" And then she listened. After that she checked on me almost every day, often calling just to say, "How about a bowl of soup tonight?" or "Would you like to take a walk?" What she really meant was "Do you need to talk?"

Other than the young couple with cows, she was

mentoring a young woman attempting to leave a battering husband and moving an elderly couple from their apartment of thirty years to a long-term care facility. She had packed up their decades of treasures and debris, and left their apartment spotless. "Rita," I said at the end of the walk, "I really honor you for the way you serve people." "Oh," she answered, "It has nothing to do with me. It's just the way God calls me to serve."

What opportunities for service have been given to me?

THE VIRTUE OF SERVICE

September 18

Everybody can be great . . . because anybody can serve. You don't have to have a college degree to serve. You don't have to make your subject and verb agree to serve. You only need a heart full of grace. A soul generated by love.

—MARTIN LUTHER KING, JR.

What has been great about my life?

THE VIRTUE OF SERVICE

September 19

Him I call a Brahmin
Ever true, ever kind.
He never asks what life can give,
But "What can I give life?"

—THE BHAGAVAD GITA

*What am I called to give at this time
in my life?*

September 20

When you leave this world, material riches will be left behind; but every good that you have done will go with you.

Life should be chiefly service. Without that ideal, the intelligence that God has given you is not reaching out toward its goal. When in service you forget the little self, you will feel the big Self of Spirit.   —PARAMAHANSA YOGANANDA

*What service, big or small,
connects me with Spirit?*

September 21

ork as selflessly
as the clouds
that shower rain.

With concentration,
contentment and discipline,
with great joy and ease,
perform all your daily work.
Still your mind; have no fear.
Never invite anger.
Perform all your allotted tasks
to please the Lord.

If you serve your own Self with great joy,
then you serve the entire world.

—SWAMI MUKTANANDA

How fully do I give myself to my daily work?

THE VIRTUE OF SERVICE

September 22

e aware of me always,
adore me,
> Make every act an offering to me,
> And you shall come to me;
> This I promise, for you are dear to me.

—THE BHAGAVAD GITA

. . . All effort and exertion put forth by man from the fullness of his heart is worship, if it is prompted by the highest motives and the will to do service to humanity. This is worship: to serve mankind and to minister to the needs of the people. Service is prayer.

—'ABDU'L-BAHÁ

When I am serving, I am praying.

THE VIRTUE OF SERVICE

September 23

THE PRACTICE OF SERVICE

I seek opportunities to care for others.
Love leads me to service.
I am a giver.
What really matters is that I serve.
I find joy in service.
My work is worship.

I am thankful for the gift of service.
It makes my life a prayer.

THE VIRTUE OF PEACE

September 24

One simmering summer, I arrived at a retreat center expecting as a presenter to be given a private room. Instead I found I had been assigned a top bunk in a tiny, unairconditioned students' room with three other women with an adjoining, mildewy bathroom. On the third day of the four-day teacher training course I was giving on virtues in religious education, I found myself intensely irritable and agitated. I felt like I was about to blow a fuse. Hardly the attitude of virtue I wanted to convey to students!

During a break between sessions, I fled to the dormitory to steal a moment's peace. Thankfully it was empty. I stretched out on my bunk and asked, "God, help me to understand what is wrong with me. I feel so angry!" A gentle reply came: "All your senses are overloaded. And you have had no space for reflection."

When the afternoon class was over, I opened the door of the main building to a blast of hot air and went to sit on a small bench in a grove of trees. I attempted to meditate, going down an inner path to a meadow where I normally met a holy figure who would give me what-ever was needed. The heat was so intense I couldn't concentrate. In my mind's eye, the whole scene was scribbled over with a red marker. In despair, I started to get up to go back into the building but I saw Him beckon to me from behind the scribbles. I sat back down. He handed me a box of chocolates, waved his hand around in a grand gesture and smiled. The meditation ended abruptly. What it said to me was "Share with them the sweetness of meditation."

That evening I drove off in search of chocolate. The next day a woman from another course asked me, "What were you doing in your course today? I kept seeing people licking their fingers and wiping their eyes."

*What practices do I need in my life to create
peace in my soul?*

THE VIRTUE OF PEACE

September 25

We seem so frightened today of being alone that we never let it happen. Even if family, friends, and movies should fail, there is still the radio and television to fill up the void ... Even daydreaming was more creative than this; it demanded something of oneself and it fed the inner life. Now, instead of planting our solitude with our own dream blossoms, we choke the space with continuous music, chatter, and companionship to which we do not even listen. It is simply there to fill the vacuum. When the noise stops there is no inner music to take its place. We must re-learn to be alone . . . And yet, once it is done, I find there is a quality to being alone that is incredibly precious. Life rushes back into the void, richer, more vivid, fuller than before . . . one is whole again ...   —ANNE MORROW LINDBURGH

What gifts do I find when I allow myself time for solitude?

September 26

When speed becomes hurry, that's a poison. The day you stop rushing you will arrive.
—ANTHONY DE MELLO

The gods approve the depth, and not the tumult, of the soul.
—WILLIAM WORDSWORTH

What in my life creates tumult?
What would allow me to stop rushing?

September 27

... And the angels and grace descend by the dispensation of their Lord, for settling all affairs. It is peace till the dawning of the day.

—THE QUR'AN 97

O God! Refresh and gladden my spirit. Purify my heart. Illumine my powers. I lay all my affairs in Thy hand.

—'ABDU'L-BAHÁ

When have I had the inner peace to place all my affairs in the hand of grace?

THE VIRTUE OF PEACE

September 28

Contention does not profit a people.

—BRIGHAM YOUNG

Peace is giving up the love of power for the power of love.

—THE FAMILY VIRTUES GUIDE

Conflict when it is not resolved with violence, spurs growth and keeps life interesting.

—STARHAWK

I create peace in the world
by creating peace in my relationships.

THE VIRTUE OF PEACE

September 29

s a tethered bird grows
tired of flying about in vain
    To find a place of rest
    And settles down at last on its own perch,
    So the mind, tired of wandering about
    Hither and thither, settles down at last
    In the Self, dear one, to whom it is bound.

—THE CHANDOGYA UPANISHAD

*When have I been able to settle down
into peace?*

THE VIRTUE OF PEACE

September 30

THE PRACTICE OF PEACE

I enter the peace of reflection.
I find peace in solitude.
I move peacefully, without rush or hurry.
I trust that all will be well.
I resolve conflict peacefully.
I have a peaceful spirit.

I am thankful for the gift of peace.
It quiets my soul.

THE VIRTUE OF UNITY

October 1

I received an urgent request from a small University department to facilitate an "Open House" they were giving to present their program to the new Director of their Division in the University. Rumor had it that this was a corporate witch-hunt, that he was cutting budgets and reducing staff in various departments. I invited them to reflect on what they did best and how they could most effectively share that. A format of panel presentation and discussion groups was chosen and I advised each department member to present one aspect of their services and to share at least one story of how a student had been helped. "These are human beings you will be talking to. They all have hearts."

The day of the Open House the room was packed and the air fairly bristled with hostility from members of other departments competing for shrinking resources. One could sense that some individuals were truly "out to get" this department. I stood up, introduced myself as the facilitator for the day and in a firm voice, while making eye contact around the room, announced the virtues which would guide the meeting—respect, courtesy, honesty and tact. "These are the boundaries which will allow us to hear one another fully. I am responsible for making sure that we keep them."

The panel presentations were articulate, funny, and touching. People's faces softened visibly. Following the presentations the department members chaired small groups in which people aired their concerns and questions. There was laughter and a good deal of respectful listening. At the end of the day, enthusiasm was high for the value this department added to campus life. The new executive beamed, as if they were his private discovery and said, "An excellent Open House!" The department and their budget survived intact.

*What boundaries in my life create
the possibility of unity?*

THE VIRTUE OF UNITY

October 2

Have we not all one father? Hath not one God created us?

—MALACHI 2

... We are the fruits of one tree, and the leaves of one branch. Deal ye one with another with the utmost love and harmony, with friendliness and fellowship ... So powerful is the light of unity that it can illuminate the whole earth.

—BAHÁ'U'LLÁH

When has my awareness of unity with others empowered my relationships?

THE VIRTUE OF UNITY

October 3

And if a house be divided against itself, that house cannot stand.

—MARK 3

Love is healing, healing is love . . . when we learn to come together we are whole . . .

—ANNE CAMERON

What disunity do I need to heal with love?

October 4

A fish cannot drown in
water,
    A bird does not fall in air.
    In the fire of creation,
    God doesn't vanish:
    The fire brightens.
    Each creature God made
    must live its own true nature;
    How could I resist my nature,
    that lives for oneness with God?

—MECHTILD OF MARDEBURG

*I honor my own true nature, which is my
connection with Spirit.*

THE VIRTUE OF UNITY

October 5

Love consists in this, that two solitudes protect and touch and greet each other.

Once the realisation is accepted that even between the closest human beings infinite distances continue to exist, a wonderful living side by side can grow up, if they succeed in loving the distance between them which makes it possible for each to see the other whole against the sky.

—RAINER MARIA RILKE

What would allow me to love the distance between me and others, the space between, in which love occurs?

THE VIRTUE OF UNITY

October 6

He who experiences the unity of life, sees his own Self in all beings, and all beings in his own Self, and looks on everything with an impartial eye. —THE BHAGAVAD GITA

When you are weak enough, you let go, and that is when you find the rose, that is when you know that it is not you living your life, it's the Divine. It is not you who are doing anything. You do not exist in the way you think you do. You are a wave on the great ocean of energy and that ocean is carrying you at every moment. But you are also that ocean because being a wave, what else could you be but the sea? You ARE the rose you find, and that rose is blooming in everything, always. —ANDREW HARVEY

I open my awareness to the unity life is.

THE VIRTUE OF UNITY

October 7

THE PRACTICE OF UNITY

In the face of conflict, I stand for unity.
I trust the power of unity.
I heal disunity with love.
I honor my own true nature.
I allow the distance which intimacy requires.
I experience the oneness of life.

I am thankful for the gift of unity.
It empowers my relationships.

THE VIRTUE OF PATIENCE

October 8

Early one morning of a women's healing retreat, I focused in meditation on the ten participants. This is the meditation which came for Kathy, who was a giggler, a joker, and had never been to anything like this before. When the meditation came, I did not yet know that she was a mother, a recovering alcoholic and a survivor of childhood sexual abuse. She wept when she read the meditation aloud later that morning, and it gave her the courage to tell her story for the first time.

> The road is rough
> and I am strong.
> I am a runner.
> I have the patience
> to go through my fires
> for they are cleansing to my spirit.
> I am a warrior.
> I battle for my children
> and for the child within
> who has never lost her purity.

When has patience given me the strength to go through my fires?

October 9

. . . We glory in tribulations also: knowing that tribulation worketh patience; and patience, experience; and experience, hope . . .

—ROMANS 5

Patience may be defined as that quality of life which makes suffering creative; and impatience as that whereby suffering becomes a destructive force.

—ROBERT LLEWELYN

When I have suffered patiently,
how has my life been recreated?

THE VIRTUE OF PATIENCE

October 10

Patience, forbearance, always wins out, not anger. One who is patient becomes established in the Absolute . . .

—THE MAHABHARATA

Be humble always and gentle, and patient too, putting up with one another's failings in a spirit of love.

—EPHESIANS 4

What helps me to remain patient instead of allowing anger to carry me away from love?

THE VIRTUE OF PATIENCE

October 11

elp us to be the always
hopeful
 gardeners of the spirit
 who know that without darkness
 nothing comes to birth
 as without light
 nothing flowers.

—MAY SARTON

I patiently await new growth.

THE VIRTUE OF PATIENCE

October 12

The beach is not the place to work; to read, write or think . . . some morning in the second week, the mind wakes, comes to life again. Not in a city sense—no—but beach-wise. It begins to drift, to play, to turn over in gentle careless rolls like those lazy waves on the beach. One never knows what chance treasures these easy unconscious rollers may toss up, on the smooth white sand of the conscious mind . . .

But it must not be sought for or—heaven forbid!—dug for. No, no dredging of the sea-bottom here. That would defeat one's purpose. The sea does not reward those who are too anxious, too greedy, or too impatient. To dig for treasures shows not only impatience and greed, but lack of faith. Patience, patience, patience, is what the sea teaches. Patience and faith. One should lie empty, open, choiceless as a beach—waiting for a gift from the sea.   —ANNE MORROW LINDBURGH

*What would help me to await the gifts
of my life with patience?*

THE VIRTUE OF PATIENCE

October 13

Forebearing patience is the highest devotion.
—THE DHAMMAPADA 14

For everything there is a sign. The sign of love is fortitude under My decree and patience under My trials.

—BAHÁ'U'LLÁH

Be patient under all conditions, and place your whole trust and confidence in God.
—BAHÁ'U'LLÁH

*When has patience given me complete
confidence that life was unfolding
as it should?*

THE VIRTUE OF PATIENCE

October 14

THE PRACTICE OF PATIENCE

I have the patience to endure my tests.
I see the gifts in suffering.
I am patient with others.
I am hopeful and expectant.
I wait patiently for the gifts of life to unfold.
I have trust and confidence in my Creator.

I am thankful for the gift of patience.
It gives me hope.

THE VIRTUE OF WONDER

October 15

Some friends invited me to their annual family berry-picking expedition near the border between British Columbia and Alaska. We slept in tents under a star-filled sky. After a sizzling breakfast cooked over an open fire, we climbed up the gentle mountain slope. As if by a silent, predetermined command, each of us drifted off to find a solitary patch of blueberries out of view of the others. The morning mist had lifted and the spot on which I sat was already warm. I took off my sweater and felt the sunny air on my bare arms. I breathed in the loamy scent of warm earth mixed with sweet pine and berries. I leaned into the gentle slope, legs curled to the side, welcomed by the slight hollow as if I belonged exactly there. The sweetly tart taste of the berries was on my lips. I was very still except for the motion of my fingers, which were already stained blue and slightly sticky. I felt I could pick for hours. The simple act of loosening berries which were ripe and ready was mesmerizing. They yielded to a slight touch, no stickers for protection. There was no sound except for an occasional murmur from friends at a distance and the light breeze ruffling my hair. My mind was so quiet. The solitude soaked into my parched soul. I stopped for a moment and looked up, breathing it all in. I turned my head and saw a panorama of mountains, snow-capped, glistening in the sunlight. I was overcome by the wonder of being so utterly immersed in beauty. Life felt seamless.

Where have I experienced wonder?

October 16

Every blade of grass has its Angel that bends over it and whispers, "Grow, grow."

—THE TALMUD

Nobody sees a flower—really—it is so small it takes time—we haven't time—and to see takes time, like to have a friend takes time. If you take a flower in your hand and really look at it, it's your world for the moment.

—GEORGIA O'KEEFE

I allow time for wonder.

THE VIRTUE OF WONDER

October 17

o know the Earth on
a first-name basis
    You must know the meaning of river stones first.
    Find a place that calls to you and there
    Lie face down in the grass until you feel
    Each plant alive with the mystery of beginnings.

                            —NANCY WOOD

*What have been the most
wonderful experiences in my life?*

October 18

Wonder is the basis of worship.

—THOMAS CARLYLE

The highest point a man can attain is not Knowledge, or Virtue, or Goodness, or Victory, but something even greater, more heroic and more despairing: Sacred Awe!

—NIKOS KAZANTZAKIS

What would allow me to see life, not as an unending series of problems to be solved, but as a mystery to be lived?

October 19

O friend, the heart is the dwelling of eternal mysteries, make it not the home of fleeting fancies; waste not the treasure of thy precious life in employment with this swiftly passing world. Thou comest from the world of holiness—bind not thine heart to the earth; thou art a dweller in the court of nearness—choose not the homeland of the dust.

—BAHÁ'U'LLÁH

Until we accept the fact that life itself is founded in mystery, we shall learn nothing.

—HENRY MILLER

What attachments do I need to release to engage in real life?

October 20

Stand in awe, and sin not; commune with your own heart, and in your chamber, and be still.

—BOOK OF COMMON PRAYER, PSALM 4

The fairest thing we can experience is the mysterious. It is the fundamental emotion which stands at the cradle of true art and true science. —ALBERT EINSTEIN

In the stillness of prayer,
I discover the wonders within me.

THE VIRTUE OF WONDER

October 21

THE PRACTICE OF WONDER

I allow myself to taste life's wonders.
I take time to contemplate beauty.
I go to wonderful places.
I have a sense of the sacred.
I free my mind from fleeting attachments.
Communion brings out the wonders in me.

I am thankful for the gift of wonder.
It awakens my soul.

THE VIRTUE OF DILIGENCE

October 22

When Saidie Patterson was twelve, her mother died in childbirth because the family could not afford the doctor's five dollar fee. "As I stood in my dear mother's blood, I didn't shed a tear, but I felt a cross being put on my back and, at the same time, I felt a strange warmth coming into the room. Looking back now I am convinced it was the Holy Spirit. From that day on I put my hand to doing what I could for what was right, and the good Lord has honoured the bargain that was made at my mother's bedside. That night I became an adult." Saidie was left to look after the baby, six other siblings and her step-father, who became an invalid as a result of the shock of his wife's death. She also became the breadwinner, working in a linen mill.

Saidie grew up to become a union leader and a peace-maker. She led marches by the women of Ireland to end the violence between Catholics and Protestants. She became an intrepid mediator, welcomed by both sides in the conflict. She never stopped building bridges for what she believed in. . . "Peace is not going to be achieved either by the politicians or the army. It is going to be done by personal contact. That is what I believe in." Even in her late seventies, crippled with arthritis, she attended four or five meetings a week. "I'm all right from the neck up," she would joke. All her life, she worked by the words she had heard her mother say so often in the family prayer circle: "If you see something wrong in this world and do nothing about it, you are committing a crime against the whole of humanity."

Adapted from *All Her Paths Are Peace* by Michael Henderson

What goal is worthy of my energy?

THE VIRTUE OF DILIGENCE

October 23

Your time . . . is property that belongs to the Lord . . . and if [you] do not make good use of it [you] shall be held accountable.
—BRIGHAM YOUNG

If an artist does not spring to his work as a soldier to the breach, if once within the crater he does not labour as a miner buried in the earth, if he contemplates his difficulties instead of conquering them one by one, the work remains unachieved, production becomes impossible, and the artist assists the suicide of his own talent . . . The solution of the problem can be found only through incessant and sustained work.
—HONORE DE BALZAC

How diligently am I using my time?

THE VIRTUE OF DILIGENCE

October 24

We are the trees of My garden; ye must give forth goodly and wondrous fruits, that ye yourselves and others may profit therefrom. Thus it is incumbent on every one to engage in crafts and professions, for therein lies the secret of wealth . . . .

—BAHÁ'U'LLÁH

God is glorified in the fruitage of our lives.   —JOEL S. GOLDSMITH

What is the fruitage of my life?

October 25

omorrow God isn't
going to ask
  What did you dream?
  What did you think?
  What did you plan?
  What did you preach?
  He's going to ask What did you do?

—MICHEL QUOIST

What dreams am I ready to put into action?

October 26

Even the wise man acts in character with his nature; indeed, all creatures act according to their natures. What is the use of compulsion then? —THE BHAGAVAD GITA 3

In the story of the Ugly Duckling when did the Ugly Duckling stop feeling Ugly? When he realized that he was a Swan. Each of us has something Special, a Swan of some sort, hidden inside somewhere. But until we recognize that it's there, what can we do but splash around, treading water? The Wise are Who They Are. They work with what they've got and do what they can do. —BENJAMIN HOFF

When do I get caught up in compulsion and
inadequacy, rather than working
with what I have?

October 27

I hope you will go out and let stories, that is life, happen to you, and that you will work with these stories from your life— your life, not someone else's life—water them with your blood and tears and your laughter till they bloom, till you yourself burst into bloom. That is the work. The only work.

—CLARISSA PINKOLA ESTÉS

*When do I most allow
my own nature to flower?*

THE VIRTUE OF DILIGENCE

October 28

THE PRACTICE OF DILIGENCE

I set worthy goals.
I make good use of my time.
I work with an attitude of reverence.
I am a person of action.
I do what I can do.
Spiritual growth is my true work.

I am thankful for diligence.
It energizes my soul.

THE VIRTUE OF RIGHTEOUSNESS

October 29

Mark Twain's wonderful character Huckleberry Finn was portrayed as a rascal, going up against the standards of civilized people of the American south of that time. He plays hookey from school, avoids church as though it were "pison," gets other people to do his work, and steals a slave named Jim, who happens to be his friend. Then, Huck begins to experience pangs of guilt over helping Jim escape. "My conscience got to stirring me up hotter and hotter than ever, until at last I says to it, 'Let up on me—it ain't too late yet—I'll paddle ashore at first light and tell.'" And so Huck resolves to turn in his friend, Jim. At dawn he gets in the canoe and tells Jim he is just going to check on their location. He paddles off "all in a sweat to tell on him."

"Right then along comes a skiff with two men in it with guns, and they stopped and I stopped. One of them says, 'What's that yonder?'

'A piece of raft,' I says.

'Do you belong on it?'

'Yes, sir.'

'Any men on it?'

'Only one, sir.'

THE VIRTUE OF RIGHTEOUSNESS

'Well, there's five niggers run off tonight up yonder, above the head of the bend. Is your man white or black?'

I didn't answer up prompt. I tried to, but the words wouldn't come.

I tried for a second or two to brace up and out with it, but I warn't man enough—hadn't the spunk of a rabbit. I see I was weakening; so I just give up trying, and says:

'He's white.'

—EXCERPT FROM *HUCKLEBERRY FINN* BY MARK TWAIN

When have I listened to what my heart knew was right?

THE VIRTUE OF RIGHTEOUSNESS

October 30

Clothe thyself with the essence of righteousness, and let thine heart be afraid of none except God.

—BAHÁ'U'LLÁH

One righteous act . . . hath the power to restore the force that hath spent itself and vanished . . . .

—BAHÁ'U'LLÁH

When have I been empowered to do the right thing, regardless of the opinions of others?

October 31

And can any of you by worrying add a single hour to your span of life? . . . Consider the lilies of the field, how they grow; they neither toil nor spin, yet I tell you, even Solomon in all his glory was not clothed like one of these. But if God so clothes the grass of the field, which is alive today and tomorrow is thrown into the oven, will he not much more clothe you— you of little faith? Therefore, do not worry, saying "What will we eat?" or "What will we drink?" or "What will we wear?" . . . indeed your heavenly Father knows that you need all these things. But strive first for the kingdom of God and his righteousness, and all these things will be given to you as well. —MATTHEW 6

What would allow me to replace worry with trust?

THE VIRTUE OF RIGHTEOUSNESS

November 1

Righteousness is one thing, self-righteousness is another. May God keep me from ever confusing them.

—RABBI LIONEL BLUE

You judge others because you judge yourself. Since you judge yourself you assume others are judging you. So you point to another to divert attention away from you. Learn not to judge yourself, and it will not occur to you to judge another.

—TOLBERT MCCARROLL

How can I distinguish between being righteous and being self-righteous?

November 2

Does not wisdom call,
and does not understanding raise her voice? . . .
All the words of my mouth are righteous;
there is nothing twisted or crooked in them . . .
The fear of the Lord is hatred of evil.

—PROVERBS 8

He restoreth my soul:
He leadeth me in the paths of righteousness for
his name's sake. —PSALM 23

*Creator, help me to walk away from what is
destructive to my spirit. Restore my soul and
lead me to the path that is right for me.*

November 3

So let us not grow weary in doing what is right, for we will reap at harvest time, if we do not give up. So then, whenever we have an opportunity, let us work for the good of all . . .

—GALATIANS 6

Like all revolutions, guerrilla goodness begins slowly, with a single act. Let it be yours.

—GLAMOUR MAGAZINE

When have I done the right thing,
even though I felt like giving up?

November 4

THE PRACTICE OF RIGHTEOUSNESS

I listen to my heart.
Integrity leads me to do what is right.
I seek first what feels right in my soul. Every
    thing else follows.
I have no need to judge myself or others.
I stay clear of evil influences.
I will never give up.

I am thankful for righteousness.
It restores my soul.

THE VIRTUE OF FLEXIBILITY

November 5

It is said that you teach what you most need to learn. One afternoon during a "Healing for the Healers" retreat I was facilitating for First Nations caregivers in Northern Canada, we took a "spirit walk," contemplating something in Nature which spoke to each of us and the virtue of which it spoke. I walked slowly down to the lake, breathing in the fresh summer air. After a few minutes, what caught my eye was a slender herb about eight inches high with a tiny tassel at the top that waved in the breeze. I hunkered down to take a closer look. To my surprise, when the wind blew harder, it moved in a full circle—all the way around—then returned to its upright position. I thought, "what flexibility!" I tugged gently and then harder and found it to be firmly rooted. It was very strong, steadfast, yet it moved so freely.

When I returned to the lodge, I partnered with an elder, and we shared our experiences during the Spirit Walk. While I was sharing, she said "Something touched you about that little reed. What was it?" "The way it could move all the way around!" In the warmth of her compassionate gaze, my eyes filled with tears as I thought of the relationship which needed healing in my life. My pain melted in the safety of her reverent silence. Then she said, "Don't worry, Linda. Just like that strong little reed, you'll find a way around it."

What issue in my life has been resolved through finding a way around it?

November 6

If it be Thy pleasure, make me to grow as a tender herb in the meadows of Thy grace, that the gentle winds of Thy will may stir me up and bend me into conformity with Thy pleasure in such wise that my movement and my stillness may be wholly directed by Thee.

—BAHÁ'U'LLÁH

Is it time for me to move or to be still?

November 7

A man should endeavour to be as pliant as a reed, yet hard as cedar wood.

—THE TALMUD

I bend but do not break.

—JEAN DE LA FONTAINE

Before what challenge in my life do I need to bend without breaking?

November 8

Do I contradict myself?
Very well then I contradict myself,
(I am large, I contain multitudes).

—WALT WHITMAN

Life is a wave, which in
no two consecutive moments of its existence is
composed of the same particles.

—JOHN TYNDALL

*How well do I give myself permission to
change my mind, to go with the flow?*

THE VIRTUE OF FLEXIBILITY

November 9

I learned, when hit by loss, to ask the right question: "What next?" instead of "Why me?"

... Whenever I am willing to ask "What is necessary next?" I have moved ahead. Whenever I have taken no for a final answer I have stalled and gotten stuck. I have learned that the key to career resiliency is self-empowerment and choice.

—JULIA CAMERON

Creator, help me to find my resilience,
to listen with clarity to what is next.

THE VIRTUE OF FLEXIBILITY

November 10

A happy and gracious flexibility," Pericles calls this quality . . . lucidity of thought, clearness and propriety of language, freedom from prejudice and freedom from stiffness, openness of mind, amiability of manners.

—MATHEW ARNOLD

What gifts have I received from flexibility?

THE VIRTUE OF FLEXIBILITY

November 11

THE PRACTICE OF FLEXIBILITY

I find creative ways to resolve problems.
I discern when to be still and when to act.
My strength is rooted in flexibility.
I go with the flow.
I have the resilience to learn from my losses.
I am gracious with others.

I am thankful for flexibility.
It keeps my spirit supple.

THE VIRTUE OF MODERATION

November 12

I knew I needed to get away—alone. There had been too much work, too many trips that year. I was unable to find sanctuary at home, with administrivia piling up ominously in the office, barricading my overloaded mind from needed rest. It took me days to summon the courage to tell my husband what I had decided to do. Finally, one morning, I took a deep breath and went over to his desk. I asked him to come and look at the annual calendar we had on our office wall. There were hardly any spaces left, except in July. As a tear slid silently down my face, I said, "I have been thinking. I'm starting to burn out on all this work and travel. I want to go away in July, for a couple of weeks. And, Sweetheart, I need to do it alone. I want to visit Barbara at her wilderness cabin." This would have been the first time we had not spent our whole holiday time together. He looked stunned, and after a long silence said, "Do what you have to do."

That summer, my soul and body were restored by the starry silence, the mountain vistas, the morning mist rising off the lake with only the sound of the loons, the gliding of Barbara's little boat on aqua blue glacial water, the taste of fresh-caught Grayling cooked over a driftwood fire, the laughter and mostly the silence in the presence of my friend to whom I had no ties of responsibility, the time for unhurried, unharried prayer. It is now a regular pilgrimage, and my husband has happily created one of his own. How thankful I am for having found a way to restore balance to my soul.

What activities restore my soul and sustain the balance in my life?

THE VIRTUE OF MODERATION

November 13

e his
My special thanks, whose even-balanced soul,
From first youth tested up to extreme old age,
Business could not make dull, nor passion wild:
Who saw life steadily and saw it whole.

—MATTHEW ARNOLD

*What helps me to balance business
and pleasure?*

November 14

Anything alive that makes demands, arouses in me an infinite capacity to give it its due, the consequences of which completely use me up. —RAINER MARIA RILKE

Easy does it.
—ALCOHOLICS ANONYMOUS SLOGAN

What limits do I need to set so that I will not be used up by the demands of my life?

November 15

He who lives without looking for pleasures, his senses well controlled, moderate in his food, faithful and strong, him. . . (the temptor) will certainly not overthrow, any more than the wind throws down a rock mountain.

—THE DHAMMAPADA 8

Moderation helps me to control my senses.
My senses do not control me.

THE VIRTUE OF MODERATION

November 16

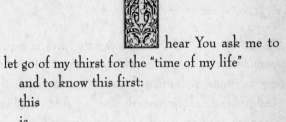I hear You ask me to
let go of my thirst for the "time of my life"
and to know this first:
this
is
the time of my life.

—KATHLEEN M. HENRY

When am I most able to let go of a craving
for more and relish the fact
that this is my life?

THE VIRTUE OF MODERATION

November 17

How often has it happened that an individual who was graced with every attribute of humanity and wore the jewel of true understanding, nevertheless followed after his passions until his excellent qualities passed beyond moderation and he was forced into excess . . . A good character is in the sight of God . . . and the possessors of insight, the most excellent and praiseworthy of all things, but always on the condition that its center of emanation should be reason and knowledge and its base should be true moderation.

Moderation is the silken string running through the pearl chain of all virtues.

—JOSEPH HALL

*How does being moderate help me
to sustain my other virtues?*

THE VIRTUE OF MODERATION

November 18

THE PRACTICE OF MODERATION

I take time for recreation.
I keep life in perspective.
I set respectful limits.
I am moderate with my appetites.
I release craving and enjoy what is.
I give up excess, even with my virtues.

I am thankful for moderation.
It is the steward of my soul.

THE VIRTUE OF KINDNESS

November 19

My son, Craig, was born too early. His lungs collapsed soon after he was born. I could hardly bear to look at his tiny five-pound body struggling to breathe in the incubator in which he was placed beyond the nursery glass. In the room I shared with another young mother, I grieved quietly, a stream of people I didn't know coming and going, barking, prophesying, talking at me. "Stop your crying. It won't help your son," one nurse commanded. "He has a 12% chance of making it," said one doctor. "We're doing all we can. He should be just fine," the next one said. Meanwhile, my husband and I weren't allowed near the baby. I felt afraid, isolated, confused.

When the nurse wheeled in my roommate's baby, the sounds of her nursing and cooing to him were more than I could bear. I fled to an empty lounge and prayed my sadness and anger, finally releasing the tears I had held back. A strange tenderness settled over me and I heard a voice say, "What's wrong, little mother?" I looked up into the soft brown eyes of an elderly man leaning on a broom. "My baby might not live, but they're not sure." "Mm, Mm, Mm." he murmured, shaking his head. He smiled at me and went on with his work.

THE VIRTUE OF KINDNESS

I returned to my room, got into bed and drifted off to sleep. About an hour later, I awoke to a gentle touch on my shoulder. A nurse's aide said, "Time for juice, dear." She was a motherly looking woman, plump and rosy-cheeked. She smiled into my eyes and in a soft tone, said "You seem real sad. Do you need to talk?" She sat on the edge of the bed and stroked my hand as I cried. "I'm afraid he might die without a mother's touch," I said. "Do you want me to touch him for you?" she asked. My son remained in an incubator for three weeks. As hospital staff, Marie was permitted where I was forbidden to go. Waiting for our baby to come home, I was comforted by the assurance that Marie was giving him regular doses of love.

*When have small kindnesses made a
big difference in my life?*

THE VIRTUE OF KINDNESS

November 20

As the vital rays of the sun nurture all, so should you spread rays of hope in the hearts of the poor and forsaken, kindle courage in the hearts of the despondent, and light a new strength in the hearts of those who think they are failures. When you realise that life is a joyous battle of duty and at the same time a passing dream, and when you become filled with the joy of making others happy by giving them kindness and peace, in God's eyes your life is a success.

—PARAMAHANSA YOGANANDA

In my picture of success,
what part does kindness play?

THE VIRTUE OF KINDNESS

November 21

Spread love everywhere you go: first of all in your own house. Give love to your children, to your wife or husband, to a next door neighbour . . . Let no one ever come to you without leaving better and happier. Be the living expression of God's kindness; kindness in your face, kindness in your eyes, kindness in your smile, kindness in your warm greeting.

—MOTHER TERESA

If we fail to feed the needy, we do not have God's love, no matter what we say. Regardless of what we do or say at 11 am on a Sunday morn, affluent people who neglect the poor are not people of God.

—RONALD SIDER

There are so many opportunities to be kind. Today, I plan to take advantage of them.

November 22

Hesitation and restraint make altruism and kindness possible.

—JUNE JORDAN

There is a grace of kind listening as well as a grace of kind speaking.

—ANONYMOUS

*What helps me to have the self-restraint to
listen and speak with kindness?*

THE VIRTUE OF KINDNESS

November 23

oving kindness is greater than laws; and the charities of life are more than all ceremonies. —THE TALMUD

he heart benevolent and kind
The most resembles God.

—ROBERT BURNS

Who is the most charitable person I know?

THE VIRTUE OF KINDNESS

November 24

. . . Upon the interconnection of all parts of the world-tree, dependeth the flourishing of leaf and blossom . . . For this reason must all human beings powerfully sustain one another . . .

Let them purify their sight and behold all humankind as leaves and blossoms and fruits of the tree of being. Let them at all times concern themselves with doing a kindly thing for one of their fellows, offering to someone love, consideration, thoughtful help.

—'ABDU'L-BAHÁ

How far do I reach out in kindness?

THE VIRTUE OF KINDNESS

November 25

THE PRACTICE OF KINDNESS

I offer small kindnesses that make a big
  difference.
I am a success when I am kind.
I take the opportunities I am given to be kind.
I have the self-discipline to communicate
  kindly.
Kindness is a priority in my life.
I keep thoughtfulness in mind.

*I am thankful for the gift of kindness.
It opens my heart to others.*

THE VIRTUE OF ORDER

November 26

I have faced my fear of heights by climbing mountains, feel energized by speaking to large audiences, gladly take financial risks for the sake of a worthy venture and regularly take on my personal dragons. What sets my heart to fibrillating and weakens my knees is adminophobia—the fear of all the little tasks undone that grow like mold, that mock and whine, "You're not enough. You'll never get done." One morning after returning from a trip, an anxiety attack woke me early. Bleary-eyed, I got up and went to my prayer corner. "Help!" I said aloud, "I need real help! I just can't face the pile on my desk." I saw in my mind's eye a holy figure in the distance standing on a beach where I often saw him. He was smiling at me and beckoning. As I approached him, I noticed something colorful in his right hand, glinting in the sunlight. It was a set of "pick-up sticks," a game I played as a child. He lifted his head and raised his eyebrows, directing me to watch closely. He tossed the sticks onto the sand where they landed in a jumbled pile. He put his thumb and forefinger together and shook them with a wry expression which said "Watch this!" He bent slightly from the waist, and, without disturbing the rest of the pile, carefully and effortlessly picked up one red stick. He held it up with a triumphant smile and looked deep into my eyes. I quickly journaled the meditation, writing "One thing at a time."

When I walked into the office, there was the expected pile left by my secretary. As my computer hummed to life, I picked up one thing from the teetering pile with thumb and forefinger. I handled it with calm, focused concentration. By noon, my out-basket was brimming and my desk was mercifully clear.

What simple method would create order in my work?

THE VIRTUE OF ORDER

November 27

Thus saith the Lord:
Set thy house in order.

—1 KINGS 20

Order and simplification are the first steps toward the mastery of a subject—the actual enemy is the unknown.

—THOMAS MANN

In what areas of my life do I need to simplify and create order?

THE VIRTUE OF ORDER

November 28

God is not found in the soul by adding anything, but by a process of subtraction.

—MEISTER ECKHART

Order is not pressure which is imposed on society from without, but an equilibrium which is set up from within.

—JOSÉ ORTEGA Y GASSET

*What do I need to subtract in my life
in order to live soulfully?*

THE VIRTUE OF ORDER

November 29

She would greet us pleasantly, and immediately she seemed to surround the chaotic atmosphere of morning strife with something of order, of efficient and quiet uniformity, so that one had the feeling that life was small and curiously ordered.

—MERIDEL LESUEUR

Chaos dissipates as I create quiet, efficient order today.

November 30

lory be to God for
dappled things—
   For skies of couple-colour as a brindled cow;
   For rose-moles all in stipple upon trout that
swim;
   Fresh-firecoal; chestnut-falls; finches' wings;
   Landscape plotted and pieced—fold, fallow,
and plough;
   And all trades, their gear and tackle and trim.
   All things counter, original, spare, strange;
   Whatever is fickle, freckled (who knows how?)
   With swift, slow; sweet, sour; adazzle, dim;
   He fathers-forth whose beauty is past change:
   Praise him.

              —*PIED BEAUTY* BY GERARD MANLEY HOPKINS

*When do I most enjoy the beauty
and order of creation?*

THE VIRTUE OF ORDER

December 1

Thy heart is My home; sanctify it for My descent. Thy spirit is My place of revelation; cleanse it for My manifestation.

—BAHÁ'U'LLÁH

The events in our lives happen in a sequence in time, but in their own significance to ourselves, they find their own order . . . the continuous thread of revelation.

—EUDORA WELTY

What is being revealed in my life now?

THE VIRTUE OF ORDER

December 2

THE PRACTICE OF ORDER

I create order in my work.
I simplify my life.
I create sacred space by putting my life in order.
I am quietly efficient.
I appreciate the order and beauty of creation.
I discern what is unfolding in my life now.

I am thankful for the gift of order.
It brings harmony to my life.

THE VIRTUE OF LOYALTY

December 3

The young psychologist felt a tightening in his gut as he walked toward her hospital room. This was Mary's third admission, each time for a more severe battering than the last by her alcoholic husband. "How can I get through to her?" he wondered. She lay on her side, turned away from the door. "Mary, may I come in?" She turned, and managed to pull herself up against the pillow. Her face was half swathed in bandages, her arm in a cast. She managed a pained smile and he had the odd feeling she felt sorry for him. "Mary, this can't continue. Think of yourself. Think of the children." "I know, Doc, I know," she said, more to placate him than an admission of truth. "How can I get through to you, Mary? Your life is in danger, don't you see that?" He saw her mouth tighten slightly with a resolve he recognized all too well.

As the late afternoon light filtered through the slats of his office blinds, he sat leaning back in the chair, arms folded behind his head. "I'm going about this all wrong. I'm fighting her. And all she does is resist. How can I help her? Why does she put up with it?" In a flash, it came to him. He got up so suddenly the chair skittered out from under him and banged into the wall. He raced to the elevator and moments later was in her room. He tried to sound calm. "Mary, mind a visit?" "Always time for you, Doc." "Mary, I owe you an apology. I'm really sorry." She looked shocked. "For what?" "I've been wrong about you. I've been blaming you for staying with your husband, but now I see what you're doing." "You do? What . . . ?" "You're keeping the family together. You are one of the most loyal people I have ever known. You're amazing." Her eyes filled with tears. "That's all I've ever tried to do, Doc." They sat together and smiled into each other's eyes. The day after her release from hospital, Mary packed up her children and went to a shelter. She filed charges later that week.

To what am I loyal,
and when are my loyalties misplaced?

THE VIRTUE OF LOYALTY

December 4

When will women begin to have the first glimmer that above all other loyalties is the loyalty to Truth, i.e., to yourself, that husband, children, friends and country are as nothing to that?

—ALICE JAMES

In thy face I see the map of honour, truth, and loyalty.

—WILLIAM SHAKESPEARE

When have I chosen to be loyal to my own deepest truth?

THE VIRTUE OF LOYALTY

December 5

The best mirror is an old friend.

—GEORGE HERBERT

A true friend loves you enough to support you and to confront you.

—ANONYMOUS

*I tell my friends the truth and I welcome
the truth they tell me.*

December 6

he steadfast love of
the Lord never ceases,
 his mercies never come to an end;
 they are new every morning;
 great is your faithfulness.

—LAMENTATIONS 3

t is, however, only in
fidelity in little things that a true and constant
love of God can be distinguished from a passing
fervour of spirit.

—FRANCOIS DE LA MOTHE FENELON

*In what little, daily ways do I experience
loyalty in my relationship with God?*

December 7

More than all else, keep watch over your heart, since here are the wellsprings of life. —PROVERBS 4

Wouldst thou have Me, seek none other than Me; and wouldst thou gaze upon My beauty, close thine eyes to the world and all that is therein; for My will and the will of another than Me, even as fire and water, cannot dwell together in one heart. —BAHÁ'U'LLÁH

What do I have my heart set on?

THE VIRTUE OF LOYALTY

December 8

Whither thou goest I will go; and where thou lodgest, I will lodge; thy people shall be my people, and thy God, my God.

—RUTH 1

Be faithful till death and I will give you the crown of life.

—REVELATIONS 2

What is truly worthy of my loyalty?

THE VIRTUE OF LOYALTY

December 9

THE PRACTICE OF LOYALTY

I choose my loyalties wisely.
I am loyal to myself.
I am a truthful and committed friend.
I show loyalty in my daily actions.
I set my heart on what really matters.
I keep my true loyalties forever.

I am thankful for loyalty.
It is the guardian of my soul.

THE VIRTUE OF PURPOSEFULNESS

December 10

When I was six, I learned the purpose of life. Half of the families in our neighborhood were Jewish and the other half Roman Catholic. I went to services with my friends, but they merely tolerated the fact that I was a member of the Bahá'í Faith, a little known religion, and they never came to my Sunday School. They thought I was weird because I loved going to religion classes. What I loved most was that we did great art. We made murals of the children of the world. We designed one-of-a-kind covers for our prayer journals with swirly colors of oil paint in a pan of water. It was like magic to me then. But there was one problem. I was overcome with fits of embarrassment by our art teacher, Mrs. McComb, who giggled every time she spoke. "Nervous laughter," my mother called it when I complained in the back seat on the way home, my brothers taunting me with giggle imitations.

Finally, one day after Sunday School, my mother decided it was time for me to stop asking, "Why does Mrs. McComb have to laugh like that?" "I think I know why she laughs," Mother said, as she handed me an open book showing an old photograph of 'Abdu'l-Bahá, a central figure of our faith, surrounded by American children. Pointing to a smiling little girl in a pinafore with long ringlets, cuddled up beside him, she said, "That is Mrs. McComb. When she was your age, she wrote 'Abdu'l-Bahá a letter. It said, 'Dear Master, Why are we here? Love, Ruhiyyih' And he wrote her back, and what do you think he said? 'Beloved Ruhiyyih, We are here to acquire the virtues of the Kingdom. Love, 'Abdu'l-Bahá.' Perhaps she laughs because she is so happy to know the secret of life." After that, I listened for the sound of Mrs. McComb's giggles. I smiled to myself, knowing her secret.

What is the secret of life to me?

December 11

To every thing there is a season, and a time to every purpose under heaven:

A time to be born, and a time to die, a time to plant, and a time to pluck up that which is planted;

A time to kill, and a time to heal; a time to break down, and a time to build up;

A time to weep, and a time to laugh; a time to mourn, and a time to dance . . .

—ECCLESIASTES 3

What time is it now?

THE VIRTUE OF PURPOSEFULNESS

December 12

Learn to get in touch with the silence within yourself and know that everything in this life has a purpose.

—ELISABETH KUBLER-ROSS

... Everything on earth has a purpose, every disease an herb to cure it, and every person a mission. This is the Indian theory of existence.

—MOURNING DOVE (CHRISTINE QUINTASKET)

When I quiet down into my spirit,
what purpose do I discern?

December 13

This is the true joy in life, the being used for a purpose recognised by yourself as a mighty one; the being thoroughly worn out before you are thrown on the scrap heap; the being a force of nature instead of a feverish little clod of ailments and grievances complaining that the world will not devote itself to making you happy.

—GEORGE BERNARD SHAW

Many persons have a wrong idea of what constitutes real happiness. It is not obtained through self-gratification, but through fidelity to a worthy purpose.

—HELEN KELLER

What worthy purpose gives me happiness?

December 14

So long as the thoughts of an individual are scattered he will achieve no results, but if his thinking be concentrated on a single point wonderful will be the fruits thereof . . . Thus is it necessary to focus one's thinking on a single point so that it will become an effective force.

—'ABDU'L-BAHÁ

What results in my life have come from being concentrated and focused?

THE VIRTUE OF PURPOSEFULNESS

December 15

You see things; and you say, "Why?" But I dream things that never were; and I say, "Why not?" —GEORGE BERNARD SHAW

Shoot for the moon. Even if you miss it you will land among the stars.

—LES BROWN

Why not?

THE VIRTUE OF PURPOSEFULNESS

December 16

THE PRACTICE OF PURPOSEFULNESS

I am aware that life has a purpose.
I honor the seasons of my life.
In silence I discern my true purpose.
I invite God to use me.
I have a clear focus.
I follow my dreams.

I am thankful for the gift of purposefulness.
It makes my dreams come true.

THE VIRTUE OF SELF-DISCIPLINE

December 17

When my husband Dan was a young pediatric psychologist, he was asked to do an assessment on Robert, a mentally handicapped child of seven, to determine the extent of Robert's capacities. As Dan explored what Robert could do, the boy said with great pride, "I can tie my shoes. Wanna see?" For the rest of the hour, Dan sat patiently and watched as Robert went step by step through the process he had been taught. "First you take the laces in both hands like this." His tongue stuck out to the side in rapt concentration. "Then you cross them like this . . . " He took minutes for each step, his brow becoming furrowed and damp with perspiration. Then he lost the sequence. He stopped, looked up and, his eyes very round, said, "Oh, I forgot." Then, he started over. "First you take the laces in both hands like this." When the hour was up, Dan indicated that it was time to stop for today. He felt a pang of sadness as Robert sighed and laid the laces down. Robert said, "I can tie my shoes, ya know. I can."

It became Robert's mission in life to show Doctor Dan his greatest feat. Finally, Dan decided that Robert's determination deserved more. He also felt that being in his own environment might help. He arrived at Robert's house one Saturday. Robert answered the door, excitement shining in his eyes. "Today, Robert, I will watch you tie your shoes. You have all the time you need." One and a half hours later, rumpled, sweaty and exhausted, Robert completed the last step. "You did it! I knew you could tie your shoes!" Dan said. "Told ya," said Robert. Dan has spoken of Robert to audiences around the world as "a giant in the realm of spirit—a master of self-discipline."

When have I had the self-discipline to take on the impossible?

THE VIRTUE OF SELF-DISCIPLINE

December 18

Those who make channels for water control the waters; makers of arrows make the arrows straight; carpenters control their timber; and the holy control their soul.

—THE DHAMMAPADA 10

Discipline, to be sure, is never pleasant; at times it seems painful, but afterwards those who have been trained by it reap the harvest of a peaceful and upright life.

—HEBREWS 12

What acts of self-discipline bring peace to my soul?

THE VIRTUE OF SELF-DISCIPLINE

December 19

Procrastination is the thief of time.
—EDWARD YOUNG

I don't wait for moods. You accomplish nothing if you do that. Your mind must know it has to get down to work.
—PEARL BUCK

What habits of self-discipline help me to move from procrastination to productivity?

THE VIRTUE OF SELF-DISCIPLINE

December 20

To straighten the crooked
You must first do the harder thing—
Straighten yourself.
You are your only master,
Who else?
Subdue yourself,
And discover your master.

—THE DHAMMAPADA 12

I have come to think of the virtue of self-discipline as self-discipleship.

—MARIAN BOCK

*What would it be like to give up my
resistance to self-mastery?*

December 21

Only those who are pure and self-controlled can find this world of Brahman. That world is theirs alone. In that world, in all the worlds, they live in perfect freedom.

—THE CHADOGYA UPANISHADS

Say: True liberty consisteth in man's submission unto My commandments . . . Were men to observe that which We have sent down unto them from the Heaven of Revelation, they would, of a certainty, attain unto perfect liberty.

—BAHÁ'U'LLÁH

When have I experienced freedom
by obeying spiritual laws?

December 22

Hold fast to discipline, never let her go, keep your eyes on her, she is your life.
—PROVERBS 4

The fruit of the spirit is love, joy, peace, patience, kindness, generosity, faithfulness, gentleness, and self-control.

—GALATIANS 5

God, help me to surrender to the power of self-discipline. I am ready to blossom.

December 23

THE PRACTICE OF SELF-DISCIPLINE

I have the self-discipline to persevere.
Self-control brings peace to my soul.
I manage my time efficiently.
I enjoy self-mastery.
In discipline, I find true freedom.
I surrender to growth.

I am thankful for the gift of self-discipline.
It is the gardener of my soul.

THE VIRTUE OF CONTENTMENT

December 24

I have thirsted for time like this for so long
cottage time, dreamtime,
my body prone and splayed in the sun.
A faint thrumming of life,
over which, blessedly, I have no control
soothes me slowly back.

The lake is too blue to look at for long.
I do not have the strength to stare.
I cannot be filled by its beauty when there is no room.
It is enough that its lappings lull me,
help me to empty the tension, which seeps into
patient sand.

Warm, lake-raked gravel re-members me,
molds willingly to my body.
Decisions knock and find no one home.
Plans are flicked away like unwanted flies.
I can't be bothered—a small miracle in itself.

This peace of mine had a jump-start the first day,
when I opened the cabin door and surprised a bear

mid-gallop.

In an instant, we were both startled out of mindless hurry.

His black, furry, hugeness, arms like a gorilla,
flushed me out of my brain hive
Having tasted freedom, I have not returned.
Nor has the bear.

Effortlessness seems to have cleared
my murky, fraught, and silted mind
like an efficient servant, so quiet you hardly know she's there.
On the third day, an idea surfaced placidly,
like a tiny, lucid bubble, rising of its own accord.
The forgotten glazed rose-colored pot sitting empty on the deck
its gift-lilies long gone,
could hold the smooth, perfect stones, my treasures,
waiting on the hearth at home for a proper setting.

A second vision came today on waking.
Two pairs of favorite summer shoes
I liked so well I bought in navy and in beige
lie hidden in my winter closet.
I had completely forgotten them.
I feel like a mental virgin.
No telling what comes next.

THE VIRTUE OF CONTENTMENT

Sleep seduces me, sometimes three times in one day.
I blush to think of it.
I stretch and sigh, too content to fetch my pole,
to try my luck, to fetch anything at all
except water in a pail.

I cannot, will not bring myself to.
I had planned to plan my life,
but find I'm too busy being.

— *BUSY BE* BY LINDA KAVELIN POPOV

*When have I received the gift
of contentment?*

THE VIRTUE OF CONTENTMENT

December 25

... Love came up to me,
showing that a contented mind is best for growth.

—THE YASNA 43

Our ability to center
comes not from our ideas about ourselves but from
knowing that wherever we are, we are on the earth,
the sky is above us, and we are breathing.

—DIANE MARIECHILD

How does contentment affect my mind?

THE VIRTUE OF CONTENTMENT

December 26

The Lord is my shepherd. I shall not want.

He makes me to lie down in green pastures;

He leads me beside the still waters.

He restores my soul;

He leads me in the paths of righteousness for His name's sake.

Yea, though I walk through the valley of the shadow of death, I will fear no evil; for You are with me; Your rod and Your staff, they comfort me.

You prepare a table before me in the presence of my enemies;

You anoint my head with oil; My cup runs over.

Surely goodness and mercy shall follow me all the days of my life; and I will dwell in the house of the Lord forever.　　　　　　　—PSALM 23

When have I allowed faith to fill my cup and restore me to contentment?

THE VIRTUE OF CONTENTMENT

December 27

... When I started this journey, I had pictures of the right way to be and the right things to do ... now this quilt, this book, this life is teaching me to trust, no matter what life turns out to be—even if it is not what I expected or what I thought I wanted.

—SUE BENDER

An elegant sufficiency,
content,
    Retirement, rural quiet, friendship, books.

—JAMES THOMSON

How often do I allow myself the things which
bring contentment to my soul?

THE VIRTUE OF CONTENTMENT

December 28

have learned to be content with whatever I have.

—PHILIPPIANS 4

estow upon me my portion, O Lord, as Thou pleasest, and cause me to be satisfied with whatsoever Thou hast ordained for me. —THE BÁB

sk not of Me that which We desire not for thee, then be content with what We have ordained for thy sake, for this is that which profiteth thee, if therewith thou dost content thyself. —BAHÁ'U'LLÁH

What has been ordained for me?

December 29

Hope is important, because it can make the present moment less difficult to bear ... But that is the most that hope can do for us—to make some hardship lighter. When I think deeply about the nature of hope, I see something tragic. Since we cling to our hope in the future, we do not focus our energies and capabilities on the present moment. We use hope to believe something better will happen in the future, that we will arrive at peace, or the Kingdom of God. Hope becomes a kind of obstacle. If you can refrain from hoping, you can bring yourself entirely into the present moment and discover the joy that is already here.   —THICH NHAT HAN

When have I been able to let go of hope, to be content in the present moment?

THE VIRTUE OF CONTENTMENT

December 30

here *is* hope. If you think you haven't cultivated all the virtues you heard about, understand, one day they will shine inside you. Baba Muktananda said: "These great qualities exist inside you. It's just a matter of time until they reveal themselves. When they do, you will recognise them immediately as your own. And then, as they begin to grow and grow and grow, you will experience contentment."

—SWAMI CHIDVILASANANDA

*Cultivating my virtues leads me
to true contentment*

December 31

THE PRACTICE OF CONTENTMENT

Beauty gives me peace of mind.
I enjoy where I am and what I have.
Faith leads me to contentment.
I take time for simple pleasures.
I am satisfied with what God provides.
I live in the present moment.
I trust in the unfoldment of my virtues.
I am thankful for contentment.
It shows me that life is gift.

APPENDIX 1
SELECT BIBLIOGRAPHY

The quotations used in *Sacred Moments* come from many and varied sources. I have relied most on the sacred texts of many of the world's religions, often using several versions of each as well as the writings of devotees of those religions. These include, but are not limited to, the following religions, listing one or two examples of the principal texts used.

THE BAHÁ'Í FAITH

'Abdu'l-Bahá. *Selections from the Writings of 'Abdu'l-Bahá*. Haifa: Bahá'í World Centre, 1978.

Bahá'u'lláh. *Tablets of Bahá'u'lláh Revealed after the Kitáb-i-Aqdas*. Wilmette: Bahá'í Publishing Trust, 1992.

BUDDHISM

The Dhammapada: The Path of Perfection. New York: Penguin Books USA Inc., 1973.

CHRISTIANITY & JUDAISM

The Holy Bible, King James Version. Grand Rapids: Zondervan Bible Publishers, 1972.

SELECT BIBLIOGRAPHY

The Holy Bible, New Revised Standard Version: Catholic Edition. Toronto: Canadian Bible Society, 1991.

CHURCH OF JESUS CHRIST OF THE LATTER-DAY SAINTS

The Book of Mormon. Translated by Joseph Smith, Jun., Salt Lake City: The Church of Jesus Christ of Latter-day Saints, 1977.

FIRST NATIONS SPIRITUAL WISDOM

George, Chief Dan. *My Spirit Soars.* Surrey: Hancock House, 1989.

HINDUISM

Bhagavadgita. Translated by Sir Edwin Arnold, New York: Dover Publications, Inc., 1993.

Bhagavadgita. Translated by Swami Shri Purohit, Boston & London: Shambhala, 1994.

ISLAM

Al-Qur'an. Translated by Ahmed Ali, Princeton: Princeton, University Press, 1988.

The Holy Qu'ran. Translated by Yusuf Ali. Oxford: Oxford University Press, 1985.

JUDAISM

The Holy Scriptures. Philadelphia: The Jewish Publication Society of America, 1956.

SELECT BIBLIOGRAPHY

SELF-REALIZATION FELLOWSHIP

Yogananda, Paramahansa. *Where There is Light*. Los Angeles: Self-Realization Fellowship, 1988.

SIDDHA YOGA

Chidvilasananda, Swami. *My Lord Loves a Pure Heart: The Yoga of Divine Virtues*. New York: SYDA Foundation, 1994.

SUFISM

Harvey, Andrew. *The Way of Passion: A Celebration of Rumi*. Berkley: Frog Limited, 1994.

TAOISM

Huan Daoren. Translated by Thomas Cleary. *Back to Beginnings: Reflections on the Tao*. London: Shambhala, 1990.

ZOROASTRIANISM

The Gospel of Zarathustra. Adyar: The Theosophical House, 1978.

I also want to give special acknowledgement to the following references, which were a rich source of quotations.

Bartlett, John. *Familiar Quotations*. 16th ed. Jus-

SELECT BIBLIOGRAPHY

tin Kaplan, General Editor. Boston, New York, Toronto, London: Little, Brown and Co., 1992.

Divine Virtues & Spiritual Qualities: A Compilation from the Sacred Texts. Salt Spring Island, B.C.: WellSpring International Education Foundation, 1994.

The Harper Religious & Inspirational Quotation Companion. Compiled and edited by Margaret Pepper. London: Harper & Row Publishers, 1989.

APPENDIX 2
PERMISSIONS

PERMISSIONS

BALLANTINE BOOKS From *For Writers Only* by Sophy Burnham. Copyright © 1994 by Sophy Burnham. Reprinted by permission of Ballantine Books, a division of Random House, Inc.

BANTAM BOOKS From *Peace Is Every Step* by Thich Nhat Hahn. Copyright © 1991by Thich Nhat Hanh. Used by permission of Bantam Books, a division of Bantam Doubleday Dell Publishing Group, Inc.

BANTAM BOOKS From *The Feminine Face of God* by Sherry Ruth Anderson and Patricia Hopkins. Copyright © 1991 by Sherry Ruth Anderson and Patricia Hopkins. Reprinted with permission of Bantam Books.

BANTAM DOUBLEDAY DELL PUBLISHING GROUP, INC. Excerpts from *Spirit Walker* by Nancy Wood, Illustrations by Frank Howell. Copyright © 1993 by Nancy Wood. Used by permission of Doubleday, a division of Bantam Doubleday Dell Publishing Group, Inc.

CAROL PUBLISHING GROUP From *Out of My Later Years* by Albert Einstein. Copyright © 1956, 1984 by the Estate of Albert Einstein. Published by arrangement with Carol Publishing Group. A Citadel Press Book.

PERMISSIONS

PERMISSIONS

PERMISSIONS

PERMISSIONS

PERMISSIONS

PERMISSIONS

APPENDIX 3
VIRTUES PROJECT PROGRAMS
AND MATERIALS

The Virtues Project offers a wide range of programs and materials for people seeking to deepen their spiritual practices; parents raising morally conscious children; schools creating a culture of character; caregivers seeking to address the spiritual dimension; organizations seeking to enhance corporate spirit.

The Programs of The Virtues Project Include:
- Conference presentations by Linda Kavelin Popov and Dan Popov, Ph.D.
- Virtues Project Facilitator Intensives in many countries
- Workshops for Parents, Schools, Corporations, and Social Service Agencies
- Organizational Consulting
- Spiritual Growth Intensives for Individuals
- Community Development and Healing Projects

The Virtues Project Products Include:
- Virtues Cards: A pack of 4"x5" cards, in full

VIRTUES PROJECT PROGRAMS AND MATERIALS

> colour, illustrated, describing each of the 52 virtues named in *The Family Virtues Guide* used in "Virtues Picks"

- Wallet Cards of the 52 virtues in *The Family Virtues Guide*
- Poster: "Virtues: The Gifts Within" full color 24" x 36"
- Little Virtues Cards reflecting the virtues in *Sacred Moments* to use for "Virtues Picks"
- Audio & Video Tapes

Worldwide Web Site:

Visit our website at http://www.virtuesproject.com

- to view a catalogue of materials and how to order them
- to peruse our global newsletter
- to obtain a schedule of all presentations, workshops, and trainings
- to find the location of Virtues Project Associations and facilitators

For Program Information:

Telephone: (250) 537 1978

Fax: (250) 537 4647

Email: virtuespro@aol.com

Orders: In North America, call 1 (888) 261 5611

In other countries, call (423) 870 3884

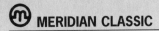

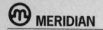

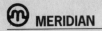 **MERIDIAN**

THE VARIETY OF THOUGHT

(0452)

☐ **EXISTENTIALISM FROM DOSTOEVSKY TO SARTRE selected and introduced by Walter Kaufmann.** Revised and expanded. The basic writings of existentialism, many never before translated, including Kierkegaard, Nietzsche, Kafka, and Camus. (009308—$14.95)

☐ **THE ESSENTIAL ERASMUS, selected and translated with an Introduction and Commentary by John P. Dolan.** The first single volume in English to show the full range of thought of one of the great Catholic minds of the Renaissance. Includes the complete text of *The Praise of Folly*. (009723—$12.95)

☐ **UTILITARIANISM, ON LIBERTY, and ESSAY ON BENTHAM by John Stuart Mill; together with selected writings of Jeremy Bentham and John Austin. Edited with an Introduction by Mary Warnock.** These essays, together with Mary Warnock's interpretive Introduction, offer a comprehensive view of the development of a major philosophical trend of Western intellectual history. (009707—$11.95)

Prices slightly higher in Canada.

MD11Y

DUTTON ⓟ **PLUME**

YOUR INNER SELF

☐ **ABOVE AND BEYOND** *365 Meditations for Transcending Chronic Pain and Illness* **by J.S. Dorian.** Daily companion that combines inspiring quotations with positive words from the author, a survivor of cancer, heart disease, and lupus. With a reassuring meditation for every day of the year, it is a sourcebook of strength and courage for anyone facing the challenges of a chronic condition or acute illness. (276268—$9.95)

☐ **BECOME HAPPY IN EIGHT MINUTES by Simon Reynolds.** Simple, powerful steps to improve your mood quickly. Drawing on a unique combination of visual-ization, neurology, spirituality, and biochemistry, this essential guide provides six simple steps to elevate your mood instantly and if practiced over time, lastingly. (274885—$9.95)

☐ **SHORTCUT THROUGH THERAPY** *Ten Principles of Growth-Oriented, Con-tented Living* **by Richard Carlson, Ph.D.** A stress consultant teaches the ten easy principles of growth-oriented, contented living and reveals how traditional therapy often interferes with the healing process. "A wonderful book of 'shortcut nuggets' that lead the way to changing our attitudes so that we may choose happiness."—Gerald Jampolsky, M.D., author of *Letting Go of Fear* (273838—$10.95)

☐ **THE IMMUNE POWER PERSONALITY** *7 Traits You Can Develop to Stay Healthy* **by Henry Dreher.** The author reveals that the key to mind-body health is not avoiding stress, but developing personal strengths for coping with hard times. We can cultivate seven traits of resilience that help us fight disease, and keep us robust and vigorous. "Excellent . . . a valuable guide to achieving personal immune power."—Bernie Siegel, author of *Love, Medicine and Miracles* (275466—$13.95)

☐ **INSTANT CALM** *Over 100 Easy-to-Use Techniques for Relaxing Mind and Body* **by Paul Wilson.** This book offers the easiest, most effective relaxation techniques ever assembled in a single volume. They include age-old methods from many different cultures, and exercises from the most up-to-date scientific research. By removing your immediate anxiety, these techniques can help you regain perspective on life as a whole, enabling you to lower your tension level for the long term. (274338—$11.95)

☐ **FACING THE WOLF** *Inside the Process of Deep Feeling Therapy* **by Theresa Sheppard Alexander.** This extraordinary book vividly and vibrantly recreates the first eight sessions in a course of therapy from the points of view of both the patient and the therapist. The method is Deep Feeling Therapy, an off-shoot of the Primal Therapy developed by Dr. Arthur Janov to allow the patient to directly confront and "go through" buried traumatic experiences of the past so as to gain freedom from their power to cripple the emotions and poison life. (94060X—$20.95)

Prices slightly higher in Canada.